Lifted to Lead

Lifted to Lead

*How a Paraplegic Orphan
Rose from the Streets
Of Saigon to Become an
American Leader*

Stefan Bean

Kathy Nash

ConnectEDD Publishing
Hanover, Pennsylvania

Th is publication is available at discount pricing when purchased in quantity for educational purposes, promotions, or fundraisers. For inquiries and details, contact the publisher at: info@connecteddpublishing.com

Published by ConnectEDD Publishing LLC
Hanover, PA
www.connecteddpublishing.com

Cover Design: Kheila Casas

Lifted to Lead —1st ed. Paperback
ISBN   979-8-9933700-2-6

Praise for *Lifted to Lead*

Rarely does a story come along that energizes your heart and soul to reach for better for others and yourself. Rarely do we hear about tragedy after trauma turned into gold and Dr. Stefan Bean's life story does just that. His story is one of divine guidance combined with love and grace for others. It's one of facing insurmountable odds, overcoming and living with joy and incredible purpose helping others. It's one you will share with everyone you know as I have time and time again. His story is the power of love to save, the power of ignoring *you can't* and *no* to fall in love against it all. His life is one of doing things outside the box and giving others a chance to be their best. It's the sweetest, grittiest, most inspirational true story I have heard in years. A must read!

—Tiffany Baggs, M.A. Education & Psychology, | Professor at IVC, Pepperdine GSEP, Saddleback College

Dr. Bean's heartfelt story of overcoming challenges inspires all of us to listen better, engage more, and take action to create positive outcomes. By reading *Lifted to Lead*, it is now evident to me why he connects so well with his students, staff, and partners. Dr. Bean has gone through so much, but he gives back so much more. Dr. Bean has so moved me. Bean's authentic communication style and leadership acumen in the work he does as county superintendent of schools. As a community, we are all *Lifted* because of him.

—Susan B. Parks | CEO, Orange County United Way

Lifted to Lead is more than a memoir. It's an honest and deeply heartwarming call for us to lean into the moments in our lives that shape us, to reflect on all those who have lifted us up, and recognize that each step along our journey is an opportunity to lift others and become a better version of ourselves. Dr. Stefan Bean's story is a breathtaking testament to his resilience, faith, and the power of lifting others. Through his deeply personal storytelling and the transformative *Lifted to Lead* Leadership Framework, Dr. Bean reminds us that leadership is about listening, inspiring, and empowering those around us. This book will absolutely touch your heart and will inspire you to hold the *LIFTED* framework in the center of all that you do.

—Dr. Gloria Ciriza | County Superintendent of Schools, San Diego

What sets *Lifted to Lead* apart is its unflinching look at the core of true power: the courage to transform yourself first. With a compassionate and deeply moving approach, this book cuts through the noise of superficial management tactics. It gives you the clarity to honor every voice, and the conviction to turn heartfelt intention into measurable organizational change. An empowering and necessary read for anyone ready to find their inner strength and lead with unshakeable purpose.

—David S. Kim | Co-founder, The Bascom Group

I am honored to have been entrusted to read *Lifted to Lead*. Each chapter offers profound reflection and genuine inspiration. Through his lived experiences—both triumphs and challenges—Dr. Bean demonstrates what it means to lead with authenticity and purpose. His message beautifully illustrates that true leadership means lifting others to reach their potential and paying it forward to inspire the next generation of leaders.

—Janice Frechette-Artinger | Executive Director, Parentis
    Foundation

Lifted to Lead is a powerful reminder that the human spirit, when lifted by love, high expectations, and opportunity, can overcome almost unimaginable adversity. Dr. Stefan Bean's journey, from an abandoned paraplegic orphan in wartime Saigon to Orange County Superintendent of Schools, is deeply inspiring. His *L.I.F.T.E.D. leadership framework* offers practical wisdom for leaders who want to serve with courage, compassion, and hope. This is a book I will be recommending to educators, aspiring leaders, and anyone who needs to be reminded why every child is worth fighting for.

—Ed Manansala, Ed.D. | El Dorado County Superintendent
    of Schools

Dr. Stefan Bean—a man who defied every odd imaginable. From being abandoned on the streets of Saigon during the Vietnam War to becoming the Orange County Superintendent of Schools, Dr. Bean's life is a powerful testament to the resilience of the human spirit and the transformative power of love, faith, and perseverance.

Dr. Bean introduces the inspiring *L.I.F.T.E.D. Framework*, empowering leaders to bring hope and lead with heart—just as others did for him. The book's conclusion, a touching tribute to his wife Janet and their four children, beautifully reminds readers that leadership begins with love and service. In today's challenging world, *Lifted to Lead* stands out as a beacon of hope. It's a must-read for leaders, educators, and anyone seeking inspiration to rise above hardship. A powerful reminder that no obstacle is too great when one leads with purpose, humility, and heart. I am honored to know and serve with Dr. Bean.

—Eric Goodman | CEO- MVS, Inc. & CP Products, Inc. CIO-
    Elivation Health, LLC

Lifted to Lead delivers a powerful and deeply human story of redemption: showing how even life's most painful circumstances can be transformed through authentic, steadfast love. Dr. Stefan Bean traces his journey from hardship to humility and strength, shaped by a community of family, teachers, mentors, colleagues and friends who saw potential in him that he could not always see in himself.

With warmth and candor, Dr. Bean shares the wisdom he gained from being lifted up by those who believed in him, and he extends a heartfelt invitation to readers: to remember the people who have shaped them, to reflect on how those moments of support have formed their own leadership, and to consider how they might intentionally lift others in return. A moving tribute to the power of community, *Lifted to Lead* is both inspiring and practical, reminding us that we rise highest when we rise together.

—Ronald K. Ottenad | President of Rooted Soul Ministries and Author of *The Good Way*

Lifted to Lead is both inspiring and intriguing. Stefan Bean's story reveals how strength, love, and connection can grow from the hardest beginnings. Bean and Nash share profound lessons about resilience, leadership, and the power of family. This book is a beautiful reminder that we don't rise alone; our greatest strength often comes from those who lift us along the way.

—Allyson Apsey | Best-Selling Author, National Keynote Speaker, and Director of Client Relations at Creative Leadership Solutions

Dr. Stefan Bean's story and the *LIFTED framework* offer a grounded, hope-filled picture of leadership shaped by courage and faith. His journey reminded me not to limit myself and lead with greater compassion and confidence. It's honest, practical, and deeply encouraging.

—Pastor Navon Aikens | Youth Pastor, Cornerstone Community Church

Dr. Stefan Bean's journey is propelled by a love so unconditional that it dismantles every barrier and limitation set before it. From escaping a war-torn homeland to surviving a paralyzing injury, his life appeared shaped by impossibility. Love, in the form of Janet, rewrote the narrative. Together, they defied doctors who said parenthood was impossible. Later, they walked together, proving that love fortified by faith doesn't just help us survive the unthinkable but empowers us to rise when the world assumes we're finished. Lifted to Lead stands as a stirring testament that even against overwhelming odds, hope, anchored in extraordinary love, still wins.

—Debora Wondercheck, M.S., ED. | Founder/CEO, Arts & Learning Conservatory, Arts Commissioner, City of Costa Mesa

Dr. Stefan Bean's journey has been well lived with significant moments of affirmation and ever-increasing influence. He has also navigated times of deep loss and adversity without drifting to the more comfortable. *Lifted To Lead* is a remarkable narrative of facing adversity while pursuing one's call. I have known the author for the greater part of his adult life and find this work extremely helpful in capturing his journey while providing the reader opportunities for reflection.

—Pastor Greg Rhodes | Ministry Leader, Fishbowl Ministries

Lifted to Lead is an incredibly heartwarming memoir, with a powerfully uplifting message. Dr. Bean candidly shares his many struggles, how he overcame them with the help of others, and what he learned along the way. Yet for someone so unique and talented, the reader can't help but feel personally connected, inspired, and empowered to rise above their own circumstances as well. But not for their personal advantage. This book is an invitation to find your greatest heights by living a life of love and service for others.

—Dave Darjany | Regional Director, Foster the City, Los Angeles & Orange Counties

Profoundly moving and deeply human, *Lifted to Lead* empowers us to honor every voice, act with purpose, and elevate others. With grace and authenticity, this book reveals the faith, compassion, and conviction that define extraordinary leadership. A must-read for anyone ready to turn intention into action and leadership into meaningful service.

—Lainie Rowell | bestselling author, award-winning educator, and International keynote speaker

Dedication

From Stefan:

To my wife. You are the greatest earthly gift God ever gave me. You loved me past my scars, saw strength where I only saw weakness, and filled my life with laughter, grace, and light. Every page of this book carries your fingerprints, because your faith in me made these words possible.

To our children Sophia, Amelia, Samuel and Gabriella. You are living reminders of God's goodness and the legacy of love your mom and I built together. You are my heart, my joy, and my prayer is that you always know how deeply you are loved by your mom, by me and by Him.

Above all, to God, who lifted me from brokenness and carried me into purpose. This book is my offering back to You.

From Kathy:

I am profoundly blessed by an extraordinary family who has uplifted me through every chapter of my life. This book is dedicated to my cherished family in heaven, dad, brother, and mom, whose love for us transcended life itself. I miss you every day.

To my incredible family who surrounds me now: my two sons, Anthony and Jake, you are the very heartbeat of my existence. To my grandsons, Dylan, Dustin, and Dominick, you are the radiant light in my life. To my girlfriends who are always there to support me.

To my sister, who walks through life with an unyielding strength that inspires me deeply. To my daughter-in-law, brother-in-law, nieces, their partners, and my great-nieces and nephews, you are a constant reminder of why I will always champion our beautiful family.

A special dedication goes to my niece, Shea, who at thirty-two, bravely fought and ultimately lost her battle with cancer. Your strength, determination, positive spirit, and sheer courage continue to inspire us all, and live on in Kylee and Cole. You are, and always will be, my hero.

Table of Contents

Foreword

From the moment I first heard Dr. Bean's story, I knew it was unlike anything I had ever encountered. This is not simply a tale about hardship or survival—it's a testament to the unbreakable strength of the human spirit. To rise from the streets of Saigon as a paraplegic orphan and become a transformational school leader is not just improbable…it's extraordinary.

What moved me most was not just the adversity he faced, but also the courage with which he chose to respond to it. After life continued to throw him blows, he did not allow his circumstances to define him. Instead, he made a decision—a decision to rise, to grow, and to be an overcomer.

This book is more than a biography. It's an invitation. An invitation to look at your own challenges through a different lens. An invitation to reconsider what is possible and an invitation into leadership through whatever trials and tribulations you may be faced with. After reading this book, there's no doubt in my mind that Dr. Bean will fulfill the promise he made to his wife, Janet, to "take care of the kids."

This is not just his story. It is proof of what is possible for all of us.

–Chris Singleton, Inspirational Speaker and Best-Selling Author

Prologue

This unique leadership book is a heartfelt memoir and a powerful reminder that true leadership stems from self-awareness and understanding those we lead. It offers leaders a fresh perspective, guiding them back to the heart of leading others.

It's a true honor to co-author *Lifted to Lead* with Dr. Stefan Bean to tell his extraordinary journey from the war-torn streets of Saigon to the forefront of American leadership, as Orange County Superintendent of Schools. The heart of this book is more than a moving memoir; it is a profound exploration of resilience, purpose, and the power of human connection, all framed by the innovative *Lifted to Lead* Framework.

Each chapter of *Lifted to Lead* unfolds a pivotal moment in Stefan's life, from his miraculous survival of Operation Babylift to his triumphs over physical and emotional adversity. As you delve into his story, you will discover how his experiences embody the core values of Listen and learn, Inspire potential, Foster authenticity, Transform through hope, Empower through strength, and Develop others.

The narrative progresses, revealing how each challenge Stefan faced—from learning to walk again to finding his voice as a public speaker, forged the very principles that define true leadership. Through this powerful sequence, Stefan's journey not only inspires readers, they are also invited to reflect on these LIFTED values within their own leadership paths, making this a truly transformative read.

Lifted to Lead is structured to follow Dr. Stefan Bean's extraordinary life journey, with each chapter illustrating a core value from the

LIFTED to Lead Framework (Listen and learn, Inspire potential, Foster authenticity, Transform through hope, Empower through strength, and Develop others). Here is an overview of the chapters which follow, each tied to a leadership value from the framework:

"*Lifted from Ashes*" begins with Stefan's early life, his battle with polio, and the profound experience of abandonment in war-torn Saigon, setting the stage for his incredible resilience. (Listening and Learning).

"*Roots in Unlikely Soil*" explores his adoption into a new family and the medical challenges he faced, highlighting how these experiences shaped his character and laid the groundwork for future growth. (Inspire Potential).

"*Invisible yet Becoming*" delves into Stefan's journey of finding his voice, overcoming bullying, and building resilience, demonstrating how he navigated a new language and culture. (Foster Authenticity).

"*The Weight of Hope*" covers a major surgery, emphasizing his unwavering faith and perseverance through immense physical and emotional pain. (Transform through Hope).

"*The Crowd Stands*" culminates in Stefan's powerful experience with public speaking, showcasing his impact and newfound confidence as he embraced his role as a leader. (Empower through Strength).

The heartfelt journey lovingly paints a picture of Stefan's growth from a vulnerable child to an inspiring leader. Each challenge and learning experience contributes to the development of the LIFTED leadership values.

At the end of each chapter, readers are invited to reflect on one of these values in their own leadership, making the book an interactive and transformative experience. Strap in! Here's **Lifted to Lead.**

–Dr. Kathy Nash

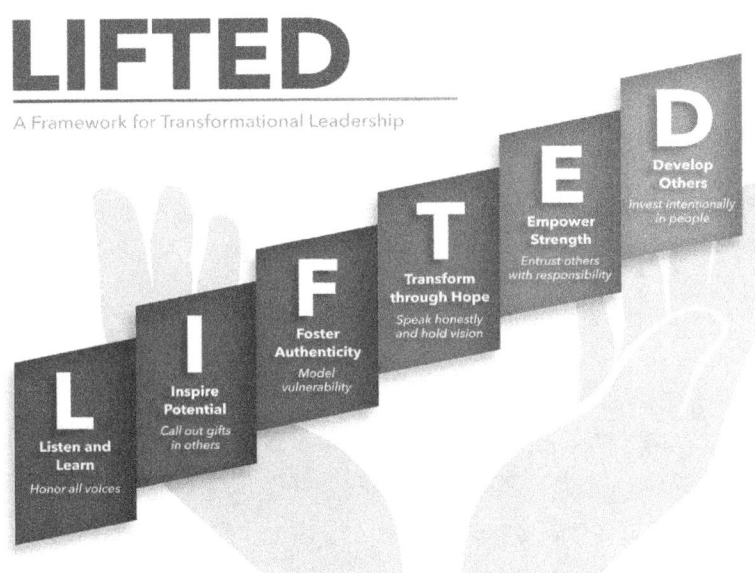

LIFTED

A Framework for Transformational Leadership

L
Listen and Learn
Honor all voices

I
Inspire Potential
Call out gifts in others

F
Foster Authenticity
Model vulnerability

T
Transform through Hope
Speak honestly and hold vision

E
Empower Strength
Entrust others with responsibility

D
Develop Others
Invest intentionally in people

CHAPTER 1

Lifted from Ashes

She wore a wrap around her head as she looked down at me. The sky illuminated from a bomb that dropped at a nearby village. She kissed me on the head and abandoned me in the streets of war-torn Saigon in 1973. I was only two, and paralyzed from the waist down. This was the last memory I'd have of my mother, and I knew I'd never get to know her or get to love her. She turned and ran, never looking back.

Don't go. Just—don't go. I couldn't say it. I couldn't move. But somewhere inside, I think I was pleading.

I've always wondered, why did she do it? Had she realized I would never walk again and knew she just couldn't care for me? Was she trying to escape as the war neared our village, and carrying me was simply too difficult? Or did she hope that whoever found me could offer me a better life then she could give me? I've always wondered how she lived with that decision—one we would both carry for the rest of our lives.

At the tender age of two, I was paralyzed by polio. I had no braces, no wheelchair, just me sitting on the street, in a corner, all by myself. At that moment, I didn't cry. I didn't move. I didn't even know how. It would take years to understand the gravity of what happened. I wasn't just left behind; I was abandoned. And yet, in the most paradoxical way, it was that same moment that gave me a future.

I sat in the cold night air unable to move, and too young to call for help. The sign around my neck identified me as Nam Le Than, a Vietnamese name that would become my past, a life I would never live again, but a life that would live inside of me forever. Not only would my name change, but I would also change. I would rise from tragedy and trauma to triumph and transformation, I would become Stefan Bean.

> I wasn't just left behind; I was abandoned. And yet, in the most paradoxical way, it was that same moment that gave me a future.

I had polio but to this day I haven't let it define me; however, it will always be a part of me. Why wasn't I vaccinated? It's a question I wish I could ask my natural mother. I would be told later that when Vietnamese babies were born, the chance of receiving a polio vaccination was 50/50. It was like drawing straws, and I got the short one.

Polio is more than just a disease to me; it's a deeply personal part of my story. As a child growing up in Vietnam during a tumultuous time, I experienced firsthand the devastating effects of polio. The virus attacked my nervous system, causing severe paralysis and permanently changing the direction of my life. For many children like me, polio was a constant threat that could lead to lifelong disability or even death.

Polio wasn't fully understood until it was officially described in 1840 by German physician Jakob Heine. By the time it impacted me, in the mid-20th century, polio had evolved into a terrifying global epidemic, affecting countless children annually.

With no cure available, vaccine development became urgent. A significant breakthrough came in 1954 when Jonas Salk introduced the inactivated polio vaccine (IPV). Later, in the 1960s, Albert Sabin developed an oral polio vaccine (OPV), greatly reducing cases worldwide.

On February 23, 1954, the first group of children in Pittsburgh, Pennsylvania, received Salk's vaccine, a moment of hope that would eventually save millions. (WHO, 2025).

Yet, these medical advancements felt far removed from my own reality. The Vietnam War severely restricted healthcare access for families like mine. Chaos, poverty, and a shattered healthcare infrastructure meant polio continued to devastate communities throughout the 1970s. Even when vaccines became available, ongoing conflict prevented widespread distribution. Local authorities tried their best to conduct vaccination campaigns, but reaching children like me in conflict zones was incredibly challenging. This painful period deeply influenced my perspective on the critical importance of accessible healthcare.

Having the physical effects of polio has obviously been a significant challenge for me. But like many polio survivors, I've also faced emotional struggles. Research indicates that emotional stress, fatigue, muscle pain, and weakness affect roughly half of all polio survivors. Other symptoms include racing thoughts and ulcers. Studies involving 2,200 polio survivors in North America revealed that 23% exhibited "Type A" behavior—driven, pressured, time-conscious, and overachieving compared to their non-disabled peers. (Bruno, Frick, 1987). Interestingly, this intense drive became a blessing for me. My perseverance, determination, and passion ultimately propelled me toward my greatest purpose: lifting and leading others.

The orphanage picked me up off the street that fateful night with only the sign around my neck to identify me. I found out later that the sign around my neck was the same sign many orphans had. Which meant we all had the same name and birth date. Nobody knew my real name or birthday. It was as if no one knew my life had started yet.

The orphanage would be my new home for now and for the next two years. All the children slept on the ground. I remember that clearly. I don't recall ever having bread or meat, just rice porridge, that was like a soup. It was up to me to drag myself around the floor and find a corner to sleep in. While this was no way for a child to live, it was the only reality I knew, and I ended up getting used to it.

I remember that I didn't bond or play with the other children. Each day was overwhelming; survival alone took all my energy. I do remember the ladies that ran the orphanage were nice to me; I can remember their smiles. This was the only comfort I knew until later in my life. Some would say my life was cursed. I would say my adversity became my strength and that strength became a blessing.

I remember vaguely that in the middle of the orphanage there was a quad area situated in the center of a small lawn. I would go there when it rained to take in the beauty and just to sit and listen. It was the only place that gave me a sense of peace. I didn't know what was yet to come, but those moments of listening taught me that even in chaos, there was something worth holding on to. My story had begun in ashes, but even then, I was learning how to rise. My personal story also intersects profoundly with the events surrounding Operation Babylift. Between April 4 and April 14, evacuations of children had begun. On April 30, 1975, as North Vietnamese troops accepted the surrender of Saigon, the United States faced one of its most painful chapters. Within hours, Saigon transformed into Ho Chi Minh City, marking a devastating defeat for American foreign policy in Southeast Asia.

I have often reflected on the chaotic images from those final days—overcrowded boats, desperate families pushing their way to the U.S. embassy, and children being handed over barbed-wire fences to uncertain futures. Those powerful moments captured the urgency and complexity of the evacuation efforts, demonstrating humanity's resilience amidst extraordinary challenges.

Vietnam emerged from the war militarily strong, but its towns and cities were in ruins from relentless bombings, and the countryside was dangerously littered with landmines. Businesses, agriculture, and industries had collapsed. The aftermath of the war was brutal, leading to mass waves of refugees fleeing the oppressive communist regime in 1975 and again in 1978. These "boat people" embarked on perilous journeys in search of safety and freedom.

My own journey was shaped by these dramatic events, highlighting the struggles and resilience of my generation as we navigated our way toward hope amidst chaos.

Quickly, in the orphanage, things began to change. Suddenly, the staff started putting me in leg braces for the first time. I remember being stood up in leg braces while they took my picture. I didn't understand then but it would all make sense later. They began taking pictures of all of the kids instead of tending to our needs, like changing our pants. I remember wondering why they weren't taking care of me or the others. That's why in some of the photos I had a scowl on my face.

I liked going to the rooftop. I remember one night I had dragged myself up there because I heard a lot of commotion. I saw military police and soldiers running through the streets. It looked like some were outside protecting the orphanage. I remember everything became quite hectic. The staff was running around, gathering things, like our belongings and paperwork. We were all ushered onto a long line of black buses. We were scared. No one told us where we were going. This was the beginning of Operation Babylift.

In Gerald R. Ford's autobiography (1975) he states, "Early in April, I directed money from a $2 million special foreign aid children's fund to be made available to fly two thousand South Vietnamese orphans to the United States as soon as possible. I ordered American officials in Saigon to cut through any red tape that might stand in the way of the children's escape. Then I told our Air Force to begin those mercy flights as soon as possible. Everyone suffers in war, but no one suffers more than the children, and the airlift was the least that we could do." (p. 252). It was Ford's vision to save as many children as possible.

That night, President Ford, Henry Kissinger and Army Chief of Staff, Frederick Weyand flew to San Francisco International Airport to welcome 325 Vietnamese children who flew in on a chartered jet. Volunteers carried off the ill, terrified and exhausted children to ambulances and buses. Ford wanted to do something for the innocent, but some media felt like it was a politically staged event. (Nesson, 1975).

Operation Babylift was a well-coordinated mission. Many agencies played important roles in airlifting orphans. The Holt adoption agency, along with a number of service organizations including, Friends of Children of Viet Nam (FCVN), Friends For All Children (FFAC), Catholic Relief Service, International Social Services, International Orphans, and the Pearl S pooled resources to make the evacuations possible.

Former Holt agency president John Williams, was a prominent figure who arranged flights out of Vietnam. His agency helped coordinate adoptive families on the US side. Three years before the evacuations, his agency was working tirelessly on placing children with adoptive families in the US. But three years later he knew there was a new-found urgency. He and the other agencies had to get these children out fast.

Holt's center in Saigon continued to care for those children amid the emergency evacuations. John had been called to utilize a USAID grant to help the children of Vietnam. He felt he had a calling to do so. In the sweltering heat of Vietnam, John set up a family assistance program that would later become a life-saving organization. John witnessed many parents relinquishing their children to the agency. The families were under a great deal of stress, and their children were suffering from poverty, malnutrition and disease. They felt Holt's agency was the answer to this. Once the parents learned that there were resources that could help them, they no longer wanted to abandon their children. They wanted to protect their families. The Holt agency gave families hope. His case workers worked with parents not only to provide much-needed resources, but to help them learn skills that would assist them in becoming independent wage earners and caregivers.

The atmosphere in Saigon began to change. In 1975 Holt had three childcare centers in Saigon. He had another center in Da Nang, the central part of the country, and a relationship with an orphanage in Vũng Tàu. He called Da Nang to check on the center and was told by a US consulate that there was no need for concern. Ten days later Da Nang was overrun by the North Vietnamese. It was time to go. (Griffes, 2025).

I remember the day we left. After boarding the black buses, we drove across the dirt fields to get to the airplanes. We were sent with our belongings and records. There were two planes leaving that day. I was set to go on the first plane, a cargo plane. Babies were strapped in boxes and children were crammed together, three to a seat with one seatbelt. My records and leg braces were put on that cargo plane. The nurses and staff members were handing babies and children over to one another and loading us onto the planes. I was terrified of the unknown, not knowing that I had a chance at a new life in the US.

Reporter Michael Rosenwald (2021), shared the story of Regina Aune, a thirty-year old Air Force flight nurse details the landing of a flight at Tan Son Nhut Air Base. "There was so much desperation." She took one baby after another to caretakers and to a new life. "You just wanted to cry," she said. "But we had a job to do." Aune shared that watching the chaos recently in Kabul airport in Afghanistan brought back these tragic memories, where babies were being handed over barbed wire by their parents. "There were parents handing their babies over to complete strangers," Aune said.

Aune shared, "When they saw me as an American, they were rushing up to me, totally desperate, just giving me their children." I went to the orphanages myself to grab children. The conditions were grim. I tripped over an infant who was stuck to the floor in his own feces. I just looked at these babies in disbelief. I spotted 20 infants and said, "I'll take them all." Aune's flight was on the cargo plane. It would be the first Operation Babylift flight, my flight. It was a military C-5 Galaxy that was unequipped for the transportation of people, let alone young children and infants. The crew secured the babies the best they could, with cargo tie-down straps.

My records and braces were loaded onto Aune's plane. Both planes were packed with infants and children then the unthinkable happened: the plane crashed.

Aune recalled the air reeked of jet fuel. The children had diarrhea and were vomiting. There was an upper deck and lower deck. Aune was with the babies on the upper deck. Older children were on the lower deck. Within twelve minutes of takeoff, the cargo door blew off, causing many of the staff and children to be sucked out of the plane to their death. Nearly everyone on the lower deck died.

There was a scramble to move the surviving babies to rescue helicopters. Aune was badly injured, but survived. Even with broken bones in her legs and feet, she drug babies in her arms. Around 130 people were killed in the crash, including 78 children. I was set to be on this plane. My records and leg braces preceded me. (p. 1-2).

The First Lady's Lady, Sheila Weidenfeld reported Mrs. Ford's reaction to the terrible tragedy:

More than 200 people were killed, the majority of them children, as the first planeload of South Vietnamese orphans bound for their adoptive families in the US. Mrs. Ford was horrified as she talked about the endless disasters and the most innocent victims of the war who were killed. Adoptive families waited to learn if their expected child was dead or alive (Weidenfeld, 1975).

I had already suffered more than most four-year-olds might in a lifetime, and that deadly flight was meant for me—or was it? By the grace of God, I was mistakenly placed on the second plane. That moment changed everything.

I had been lifted not just from a country, but from despair. Stripped of my name, my family, and even the ability to walk, I was now on a new path. A path that would be filled with pain and surgeries, but also with unexpected love, purpose, and a calling I never could have imagined.

At that moment, I didn't yet know what lay ahead. I didn't know I would be adopted by a family who would believe in me, or that I would go on to lead others and give back what I had so freely been given.

All I knew was that I had survived and somewhere beyond the clouds of that war-torn sky, a new life was waiting.

A life where others lifted me through love.

A life that raised me to lead.

LIFTED Value: **Listen and Learn** Leadership begins with listening. By listening deeply and learning continuously, leaders not only honor the stories of others but also transform challenges into opportunities for growth, resilience, and leadership.

Lifted Insight:

"I remember vaguely that in the middle of the orphanage there was a quad area situated in the center of a small lawn. I would go there when it rained to take in the beauty and just to sit and listen. It was the only place that gave me a sense of peace. I didn't know what was yet to come, but those moments of listening taught me that even in chaos, there was something worth holding on to."

Leadership Reflection: How does listening—even in silence—shape our resilience as leaders?

CHAPTER 2

Roots in Unlikely Soil

As I sat strapped into that second plane, unknowingly escaping the fate of the first doomed flight, I was leaving behind more than just my past. I was flying toward purpose. I didn't yet know it, but that moment of divine misplacement was the beginning of my mission: to turn survival into service and adversity into action.

I was crying on the flight that night, terrified and unsure of what was ahead. We landed in Hawaii before heading to our final destinations to meet our adoptive families.

A social worker who was in charge of this leg of the mission gave me candy and a warm smile. I never expected to hear from him again, but years later, when I started in my new position as county superintendent of schools, he must have seen the press release because he reached out to me with a beautiful note congratulating me.

His name is Dr. Jim Deutch. He must be in his late 70s now, but he still took the time in his later years to follow me and reconnect with me in a way that would impact my life once again. He was essential to that mission. His job was to make sure that every orphan was accounted for and made it to the right destination, and he did just that. Jim's work landed me to safety.

My life began that cold, rainy night when I arrived in Seattle, Washington. I cried as they placed me in the arms of my new mom,

Judy Bean. I didn't know my life would soon change for the better. I didn't know that I was in the arms of the person who would love me the most. I cried because I was scared and I wanted to go home to the closest thing I had to security, the only thing I knew: the orphanage. I was reaching towards the plane crying and trying to go back, but to what?

Nothing.

Take me back. Please.

The plane, the noise, the strangers all terrified me. I wanted the discomfort I knew from Saigon, more than the comfort of a new life I didn't yet trust.

Judy tried everything to console me, but I was petrified. I remember being exhausted making the flight from Vietnam to Seattle. This was the first stop on my way to Judy and Gregory Bean's house, my new home with the two people who would become my new parents. Not even a golden teddy bear from Judy, or flowers from my new sister Lauren could ease the terror. It was still there.

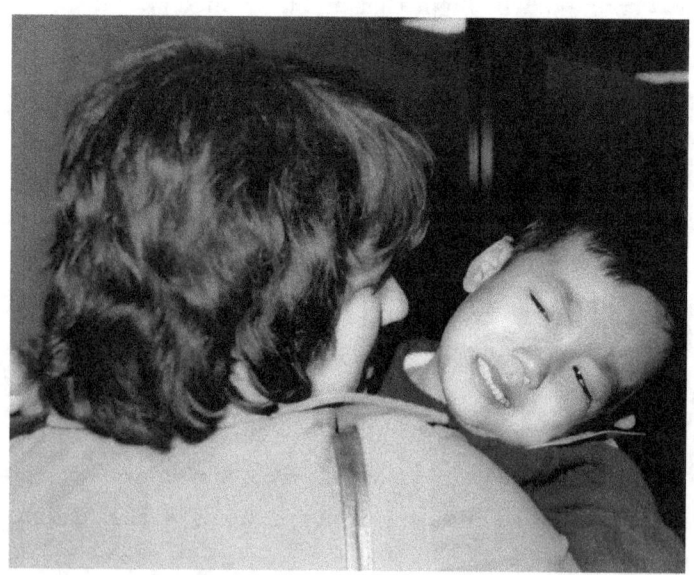

Photo of Judy Bean and Stefan Bean
from the personal photo album of Stefan Bean 1975

Three of my siblings were with the Beans. They brought the three oldest, Lauren and Darrin, my parent's two biological children, and Martin, one of the adopted children. Martin was a blonde-haired blue-eyed kid who was around six at that time, and the one I'd form a special bond with later.

Described as sleepy-eyed and unable to walk, I was one of the first orphans evacuated from South Vietnam and brought to San Diego, where I would wait six months or longer before being formally adopted. My name changed from Le Thanh Nam to Stefan Bean, and that day marked the start of a new life. That date would become my new birthday.

We boarded our final flight to San Diego. My mom and my three siblings took turns sitting next me on the plane. I remember Martin trying to carefully play with me. I thought, "Who is this kid that's trying to be nice to me? And where did that blonde hair come from?" I knew they were not out to hurt me, but I also didn't know they would become my new family; I still felt scared and so alone. Eating a banana was the only thing that calmed me.

We couldn't communicate, so there was a lot of pointing going on. Martin would point to the seat behind us at Darrin and Lauren who would point back. It took a while but I finally figured out they were trying to be nice to me. So I decided to accept my new mom, and threw myself into her arms for the first time.

When we landed in San Diego reporters were waiting on the tarmac. Being the first orphan to land from Vietnam and Operation Babylift in San Diego, I was famous and I didn't even know it.

Completely overwhelmed, I started crying again. But then the crowd of people began to assume their own identities. I would meet my extended family and many of my parents' friends. I met my first set of grandparents on my mom's side, Francis and Frank Munster, who I would later affectionately refer to as Nonie and Bachie. Then I would meet my grandparents on my dad's side, Eugene and Ruth Bean, whom

I would later lovingly call Beamie and Pappy. They were all there to welcome me, this little Vietnamese kid.

After the excitement of arriving, my family and I drove to my new home which was warm and inviting, unlike anything I had experienced before. It had a lingering smell of interesting food that had been cooked earlier in the day which I would become familiar with later.

I remember my mom took me to my room. In the middle of the room there was a twin bed. At nightfall she put me to bed, only to wake up the next morning and find me on the floor, sleeping in the corner. Dragging myself on the floor of the orphanage to a corner of the room to sleep was normal for me. This new bed was something I would have nothing to do with. She continued to put me into bed each night only to find me curled up in the corner of the floor again the next morning. It would be several months before I would actually try it out; my new-found, comfortable bed that would never be empty again.

Dr. Jim Duetch, the social worker who reached out to me recently, was also instrumental in coordinating these flights out of Hawaii. A World War II veteran, he grew up in San Diego in a house that was situated on a cul-de-sac with several other families. His neighbors included Judy Bradshaw, who would later become a double for Marilyn Monroe, Mr. Gay, and the Stephanis family. Next to them, in the nicest house in the circle was Judy Munster, who would later become Judy Bean. Jim met Judy when she was three-years-old, while playing with her brother Billy and sister Patty, all of whom were adopted. What are the odds? It turns out our paths crossed long before I would arrive in the United States

Jim was on active duty as a social worker at Hickam Air Force Base when his sergeant approached him and placed him in charge of San Diego adoptions. He would complete eighteen home studies in five days before the fall of Saigon, to urgently place orphans. Judy and Gregory Bean's home would become the model home for adoptions. Dr. Jim Deutch was the first social worker to be awarded the Humanitarian

Service Medal. Much later in life I would learn that Judy and Jim grew up together, long before I came into the picture.

> Love and warmth washed over me the night I came home with the Beans.

Love and warmth washed over me the night I came home with the Beans. It went beyond the heat from the fireplace. It was the scent of my mom's cooking, the sound of my sister laughing, and the sight of my father's smile that made me feel like I was finally home. Their love and belief in me inspired me to grow beyond anything I thought was possible. Little did I know I had just found the best home anyone could ask for.

I was home with the Beans in a house filled with love, laughter, and security–something I didn't know before but was fully immersed in now. Our family kept growing because my parents kept giving. By the end of their life they had welcomed over one hundred foster children into our home, with ten being adopted over time. I was one of the lucky ones.

Jordan and Cameron joined us next. They were twins who were premature with lots of health problems inherited from an alcoholic mother. The twins, like me in the beginning, would hardly eat. I recall only eating rice and now bananas, but our mom's great cooking would nurture us back to health.

My first years with the Beans were filled with doctor's visits. The smell of bleach and the whine of the drill in the dentist's office were a prelude to a reality I couldn't comprehend: that I would lose all my teeth.

Terrified of the next doctor's visit, I timidly entered the office, where I luckily just had an examination. I had severe scoliosis, which is a curvature of the spine, which made sitting up difficult. So many other medical concerns would present themselves like parasites, worms, and chronic diarrhea, all needing to be dealt with swiftly. From age four to eight I would undergo three major surgeries that were a result of my severe case of polio. Called "paralytic polio," it caused paralysis and muscle weakness in the legs, arms, and abdomen. The use of my arms and torso would determine my mobility, so it was important that everything from the waist-up functioned properly. I was fortunate that the muscles in my neck and throat did not cause difficulty swallowing.

While I escaped some symptoms, the ones I had to live with were severe. Fluid had built up in my lungs, and I had difficulty coughing it up. Surgery was needed to take muscles from my lower legs and implant them into my abdomen giving me the strength and ability to cough and get the fluid out of my lungs.

Even though I am paralyzed from the waist down, I discovered that I am able to move some toes on my left foot and one toe on my right; another one of God's little miracles.

Eventually, I received new leg braces and a wheelchair. I was most comfortable dragging myself around and standing up with my leg braces, so I didn't use the wheelchair often. Unfortunately, that was not enough support for my abdomen and back, so I had to start wearing a full body cast every day.

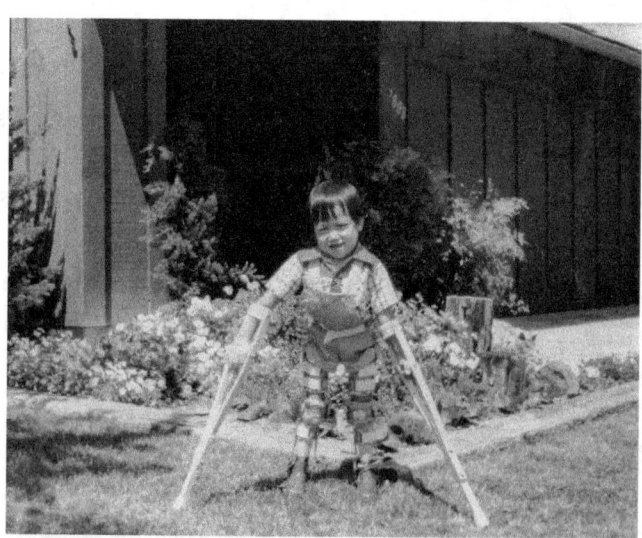

Photo of Stefan Bean in leg braces and body cast.
From Stefan Bean's personal photo album.

Our family dinners became one of my fondest memories. My dad was the head of the household and the head of the table. My parents always asked each of us to share about our experiences of the day. As our family grew, we became more diverse. Some of us were Asian, white, African American, Hispanic, and some had disabilities. The days' events were perceived differently by each of us. Our parents encouraged us to share at the dinner table. We learned to listen and value our different perspectives, knowing everyone has a voice.

Grandparents Eugene and Ruth Bean raised my dad and his younger sister Cynthia in a typical middle-class family. Dad became a sixth-grade teacher at Hearst Elementary School, who rarely mixed work with family, other than bringing home a box of papers to grade and taking us to an occasional Halloween parade or performance at the school.

He would come home each night and have a gin, while he caught up on the daily news. After he read the paper and watched the news he'd join us at the dinner table. We had our assigned seats. I remember sitting to his left. Martin, who frequently got in trouble, was on the other side of him. My dad would poke at his hand with a fork whenever he misbehaved. Dad was all about faith, discipline, and education. He taught us manners and made sure we grew up properly. He drove us everywhere and made sure we made it to every practice, rehearsal, and event. I have a great respect for him to this day.

It was only as we got older that I truly heard my dad's laughter. I now realize that when we were small, he was simply too busy, too consumed with the work of raising us, to have much time for it. He was mostly quiet and reserved, but when he spoke it was important. I will forever remember that one day he said to me, "Stefan, if you're going to overcome your disability and the fact that you can't speak English, you're going to need to prioritize education in your life." It took until about the sixth-grade for his words to sink in; it was then that I realized he was right.

17

My parents never let my disability define me. When we moved into a new two-story house, they put my bedroom upstairs. "You'll figure it out," they said. So I did. I dragged myself up and down the stairs every day. My dad also made me walk to school, five blocks on my crutches, to build my strength and character. Their tough love forged me into the man and leader I am today. But who was Judy Bean, the woman who shared this philosophy and was the closest thing to an angel I've ever known? My mom, through her generosity, would foster and adopt the neediest kids until she was simply unable to continue doing so.

My mom grew up in a lovely upper middle-class household. My grandfather Frank owned a fencing company and did pretty well for himself and his family. My mom was adopted, too, which lit a flame inside her for helping other children. She dreamed of having a large family, so after she gave birth to Lauren and Darrin and was unable to have more children, she convinced my dad to adopt and foster and he agreed. Judy wasn't complete without a large family where she could hear the laughter and voices in a house full of love. She said, "I find life is not complete without the pitter patter of little feet." She was a "traditional" mom who wanted nothing more than to be a mother and a housewife.

In the beginning, there were six of us sitting at the table every evening—but that would change. Serving us milk, salad, a main dish, and dessert at every dinner became my new welcomed normal. Because her cooking was so good, I finally started eating a lot. This was how she shared her love for us.

As our family grew, my mom spent most of her afternoons in the kitchen preparing meals for us. The meals turned into big dishes, mostly casseroles, to meet the demands of a larger family; but they were still delicious as ever. Tuna patties, tuna casserole, potato pancakes and the most amazing coffee cake, were some of my favorite comfort foods I still make today.

In Vietnam I didn't have family traditions, so adopting them was a new and wonderful experience for me. At a young age, I noticed my mother would decorate the house for every holiday, which was very different for me. For Christmas, we would rotate visits to the grandparent's homes for church and dinner. I remember the whole floor of our house was full of presents.

I would go to Pappy's house after church every Sunday where I was taught how to play cribbage. Pappy's influence would become an important part of my future. The love in our family continued to grow when baby Arthur came to join us. He and his sister Morgan blessed our house in 1981. Morgan was five and Arthur was an infant; both were African American. They came to us from a home where they suffered severe abuse. Arthur had been thrown against the wall and now suffered degenerative brain damage. He never talked and had to be fed through a feeding tube later. Mom said, "Arthur is a special angel who teaches us about God's unselfish and unconditional love. He is an incredible gift from God." I became accustomed to this new, warm and comforting life with my family. Unfortunately, tragedy struck on July 6, 1983: I started to come down the stairs. And there was mom holding the lifeless body of baby Arthur, God had taken him home, and I was devastated.

LIFTED Value: **Inspire Potential** Leaders inspire when they call out gifts others do not yet see within themselves. Inspiration awakens people to unique strengths they may have overlooked.

Lifted Insight:

"Love and warmth washed over me the night I came home with the Beans. It went beyond the heat from the fireplace. It was the scent of my mom's cooking, the sound of my sister laughing, and the sight of my father's smile

that made me feel like I was finally home. Their love and belief in me inspired me to grow beyond anything I thought was possible."

Leadership Reflection: How can you create conditions (like the Beans did for Stefan) that inspire growth in unlikely places?

CHAPTER 3

Invisible yet Becoming

Arthur's passing was a tragedy that united us in grief, reminding me how fortunate I was to be a Bean. His loss brought our family closer, and I found comfort in their steadfast support. But as I leaned on them, I was oblivious to the far greater challenges that lay just beyond the horizon.

I often reflect on the life I might have had without the Beans. Most kids with a single barrier struggle to find their footing; I was facing an entire wall of them. While the scars from those battles remain, my parents' unwavering love taught me to transform my pain into a life of service. Today, as a leader, I carry on their legacy. My mission is to give others the same grace they gave me, because the world needs more people willing to be "Beans."

One of my earliest memories with the family was my baptism on June 8, 1975, by Reverend David Laird Barclay. "We received you into the household of God," he said, planting seeds of faith that would guide my journey forever.

Despite the many challenges facing me, I knew that it was God who helped me manage and move forward in my life with love all around me. Given the struggles I endured, some might wonder why I have so much gratitude. From the outside, it seems unusual to hold such deep gratitude for a life marked by hardship, but I learned it from watching the plight of the spectrum of foster kids who came through our home. I remember the kids like me with disabilities and the kids who came from parents who were addicts.

In particular I remember Jennifer. She was four-years-old when she arrived with scars from cigarette burns all over her arms. And of course, there was baby Arthur who came to us when he was violently slammed headfirst against the wall, causing him to suffer severe brain damage. Another foster child came in with an enclave chest (Pectus Excavatum), from being exposed to alcohol in the womb. And another child with curly, red hair and glasses, Aaron, came in and was unusually quiet. He was five-years-old and had been sexually abused.

My siblings and I had seen the horrible things that were done to these children. Their trauma was so deep and their outbursts so loud that we had to experience it with them. It was difficult for us all, but because of our experiences, wonderful or challenging, my siblings and I learned to develop deep connections and empathy towards others. We became acutely aware of what we were grateful for in the midst of our own struggles.

Among the many, these few children captured my heart, making attachment inevitable, and their departure a source of tears. One sweet little baby lived with us for three months and either went back home or was adopted. She came with a statue of a baby praying. After crying for days, my mom gave it to me when she left, taking my heart with her. With the tears of sadness, also came joy and celebration when our brothers and sisters would get adopted.

Everyone who graced our household was taken care of and loved, but not catered to. We were expected to find our own way of dealing with the hands we were dealt and continue to move forward with hope. Even though I faced difficult challenges, many yet to come, I didn't have the same challenges that some of our foster kids had.

My siblings and I supported each and every foster child who came into our home. In addition, our parents taught us how to be resilient, grateful, and independent as we moved into our adult lives.

Photo of The Bean Family and Stefan Bean
from Stefan Bean's personal photo album.

My sister Lauren, who was closest to Darrin and Dad, actually had a hard time with her academics in high school, but had strong inter-personal skills and was very social. She reminds me of my mom; she had a generous heart and was more interested in caring for others than having a big career. Later on, she would care for military children, many with disabilities. Darrin, who is athletic and ambitious, would go on to earn a football scholarship to Concordia University, Nebraska. He would become a successful firefighter and rise up through the ranks as Battalion Chief.

Martin and I are close and talk often. When we were growing up Martin tried to compete for the attention of my parents which often got him in some trouble. He was very athletic too, and flourished when he went on to college, eventually becoming a successful physician assis-tant. Martin has a close relationship with his biological mom. Ironi-cally, she lives two miles from my house.

Our family dynamic changed noticeably when Anita joined us. She was an African American girl who came from a rough upbringing. It seemed that when she arrived, she often stirred things up. The first six of us were raised with firm discipline and clear expectations. My dad's rules were strict, and we all knew our responsibilities. But with Anita and the next group of adopted children, we saw those rules loosen. My siblings and I couldn't help but wonder why the newer kids weren't held to the same high standards. Maybe my dad was simply worn out by then, or perhaps he had softened over time. Whatever the reason, the shift in discipline marked a clear contrast between the structure we knew and the more relaxed approach with the later additions to our family.

The next child to join us was sweet Jasmine, also African American. She came into our world with the innocence and joyful spirit of a four-year-old, and that never changed. Though she faced intellectual challenges and had cerebral palsy, she brought a gentle warmth to our family. Caring for her wasn't always easy, but my siblings and I naturally rallied around her, making sure she felt safe, loved, and included in every way. Jasmine's presence taught us patience, unconditional love, and the true meaning of family.

Then came Jared and Jordan #2, our younger set of twin brothers. Unlike the first set of twins, who were more intellectually inclined and constantly coming up with clever pranks, Jared and Jordan #2 were on the autism spectrum with significant intellectual and emotional challenges from the start. They were premature and carried deep wounds from their early life experiences. Still, they were welcomed into our family with open arms and unconditional love. Watching the differences between the two sets of twins highlighted just how unique each child's journey was, and how important it was for us to meet each of them exactly where they were.

These were just a few of the many children who came through our home and were blessed to be cared for by the Beans. Ten foster kids were eventually adopted, while many others stayed only for a season. For us kids, it wasn't always easy to adjust to the constant transitions. Saying goodbye over and over felt like losing pieces of ourselves. Each time a child left, I would cry, grieving yet another bond broken too soon. I learned that sometimes we only get to share moments with someone, rather than a lifetime. Over time, I came to cherish every moment and every connection, no matter how brief, and to hold each one close to my heart.

I often worried that I might have to return to Vietnam. Watching some of our foster siblings return to their birth families made that fear feel very real to me. Even though Mom reassured me over and over that I would never have to leave, a part of me remained unsure.

I'd act out sometimes—not to be defiant, but because I needed to know: would they still love me if I wasn't easy to love? Would they send me back if I was too much? The fear of being returned was so deep, it shaped how I behaved, and it would take years before I could trust that this love wasn't conditional.

My parents wanted to show me through formal adoption that they were my forever family and that I truly belonged. After two long years of waiting, on Wednesday, April 6, 1977, it became official. I was a Bean at last!

Photo of the judge during Stefan Bean's adoption.
From Stefan Bean's personal photo album, 1977.

Soon after, I entered a new kind of challenge: learning to communicate. Not speaking English yet meant I had to learn the hard way, through gestures, pointing, and trial and error. If I wasn't pointing to express what I needed, my family was pointing to show me they understood. It was our silent language at first. It taught me patience, humility, and the determination to find my voice in a world that felt so new and overwhelming.

While I was navigating the challenge of learning English, my parents also wanted me to hold on to a piece of where I came from. To help me feel connected, they introduced me to a Vietnamese family in the community. I remember visiting them every month downtown, hearing my native language spoken around me and watching how they lived and celebrated together. It felt comforting and strange all at once. This was supposed to be my culture, yet it seemed foreign to me. My parents hoped these visits would help me build some understanding of my roots, even as I learned to navigate my new life and identity in America.

Around this same time, my parents knew it was important for me to be immersed in English and to experience my new culture beyond the safety of our home. So, they enrolled me in preschool. Instead of jumping in right away, instead, I watched. I watched other kids talk and laugh. I watched them paint, color, and play. I watched them interact with the teacher. I was like a sponge, taking everything in quietly. Even though I enjoyed being there, I remained silent.

Kindergarten felt much the same. I kept to myself, observing everything around me but not yet finding my voice. No one seemed to notice my silence, except me.

By the time I reached first grade, something started to change. I was finally beginning to grasp bits and pieces of English. For the first time, I felt the urge to speak up and really try. But it wasn't easy. I knew exactly what I wanted to say, yet the words wouldn't come out right. I stumbled through broken English, trying so hard that I actually got in trouble for talking too much! I didn't understand why my teacher couldn't understand me. Desperate to connect, I turned to my classmates instead. It felt like I was shouting into a void, begging someone to see me, to hear me. Even though it was frustrating, I refused to give up. I kept pushing forward, determined to find my voice and make it heard.

First grade was such an important year for me, even though I spent much of it outside the classroom. I was constantly shuttled to physical therapy and doctor's appointments. But through every challenge, my mom was always by my side. She took me to every appointment, held my hand through every struggle, and celebrated every tiny victory as if it were her own. We were inseparable, truly attached at the hip. Her unwavering love gave me the strength to keep going, and I know I wouldn't have made it without her cheering me on every step of the way.

When I was at school, I was often pulled out for speech therapy. While every service was important for my physical development and future independence, being taken out so often meant I missed valuable time in class with my peers. There just weren't enough hours in the day to fit in all the therapy sessions, medical appointments, and school lessons. As much as these services helped my body grow stronger, they also left me feeling disconnected and struggling to keep up, making it even harder to find my place in the classroom community.

Jumping in the pool with Max Jenkins, a devoted Red Cross volunteer, would challenge me to release my fears. The sessions at Children's Hospital were designed to build my upper-body strength so I could better navigate life without the use of my legs. Max didn't just teach me to swim, he believed in me. He pushed me to be stronger, to move past limits that others thought were set in stone.

In an article in the *San Diego Tribune*, my mom said, "We've been told he'll be confined to a wheelchair when he's older, but we like to think he will be strong enough to buck the odds." She also shared, "These classes will strengthen his morale and help him feel like he can do what others can do." She was thrilled that I had even started to speak a little English. (Sexton, 1975, p.1).

Max and my mom were a team, determined to help me smash every barrier in my way. With Max in the water beside me and my mom cheering from the sidelines, I felt like I could take on the world.

Back at school, all I really wanted was to feel included and find my place among the other kids. The highlight of my day was recess, the one time I felt I might have a chance to connect. Dieter, my first friend from Germany, didn't speak English either. In him, I finally found someone who knew exactly how I felt, alone in a new language and a new world.

But where there were friends, there were also bullies. Standing on my crutches, I became an easy target. Some boys would tease me by the four-square court, shouting, "You can't play sports," making me wonder if I ever would. The worst was a boy who would wait for his moment to trip me, push me, or slap me across the face. One day, as I stood at the end of the line waiting to go inside, he shoved me hard against the wall and slapped me again, snarling, "You get out of here, you don't belong here! You have chicken legs." He was pointing out what I already knew. My legs were thin and weak from muscle atrophy and the muscle transplant. For a moment, his voice drowned out everything else.

Maybe he's right, I thought. *Maybe I don't.*

I stood there frozen, not from the hit but from the echo of those words. They'd come back to haunt me in ways I couldn't predict.

I was stunned, but I didn't feel angry. The moment left a mark on me so deep that I still remember it clearly today, but back then, I didn't even know to call it bullying. Maybe I didn't understand it fully, or maybe I had already learned to expect hardship. For years, I didn't realize how much that moment stayed with me. Not the slap, but the sentence: "You don't belong here." That would remain burned in my memory. That phrase tried to brand itself into my story. And every time I proved it wrong, I felt like I was erasing it, one victory at a time. What mattered more was that I started to see the quiet strength I was building, which I believe was a resilience God was shaping within me all along.

No cruel word or shove would define me. Deep down, I even hope that boy someday reads my story and feels the weight of what he did. But for me, each bruise and each push only strengthened my resolve.

No cruel word
or shove would
define me.

My parents had poured so much courage into me that even when the world tried to push me down, I stood back up stronger every time.

There were still moments when I felt lonely, like I was watching life happen from the sidelines and missing out. But slowly, something started to change. When I finished third grade, I began to make real friends. Little by little, the other kids started to see that I was friendly and fun, and they began inviting me in.

I even started playing four squares, which was a moment that felt like a victory in itself. Sometimes I used my crutches to smack the ball, and other times I raced across the court in my wheelchair, determined to keep up. Each time I joined in, it felt like I was winning a small battle, proving to myself and everyone else that I belonged. It wasn't just a game; it was a sign that I was finally being seen and for the first time, I felt like I truly belonged.

Over time, I started to form friendships that surprised and uplifted me. One of those friends was Tim Barkett, a boy so tall he seemed to tower above everyone else. We met one day at vacation bible school, and we clicked right away.

I'll never forget one moment at church that showed me the kind of friend Tim was. There was a large flight of stairs leading up to the second floor, and back then, there was no handicap access. I sat at the bottom, wondering how I would ever get up there, feeling stuck and alone.

Then, without hesitation, Tim came over, grabbed my wheelchair (with me still in it) and started pulling me up each step, determined to get me to where everyone else was. I was stunned and, judging by their faces, my Sunday school teachers were pretty startled, too! I was so used to adults helping me, but never another kid. Tim didn't see me as different or less; he just saw a friend who needed a hand.

That act of kindness stayed with me forever. It taught me what it means to truly walk (or in his case, climb) alongside someone facing obstacles. Even now, as a leader, I think of Tim's example and try to embody that same spirit of courage and heart.

School slowly started to make sense to me. I began to realize that maybe I wasn't so alone after all and that I wasn't the only one facing challenges. One moment that changed everything was when a Paralympian came to visit our school. He was in a wheelchair, too, but instead of seeing limits, I saw pure strength and confidence.

I watched in awe as he went out to the track and raced the other kids, leaving them behind and showing everyone just how fast and fearless he could be. For the first time, I saw that someone in a wheelchair could be not only accepted, but also admired. I thought, *I can be cool in a wheelchair, too.*

He didn't just inspire me that day; he stayed connected with me, taking me on field trips and showing me a world I hadn't imagined for myself yet. I remember watching him drive a car with hand controls and thinking, *Someday, I'm going to do that, too.*

It was in those moments that something inside me shifted. I started to believe that maybe my story could look different than I had ever dared to dream.

As I became more comfortable at school, I started to notice something new: girls. I wasn't sure I would really have a girlfriend. Part of me wondered if anyone would look past my braces and scars. That didn't stop my heart from hoping.

By fifth grade, it had become a bit of a fad for kids to ask each other to "go steady," even if none of us really knew what that meant. I decided to try my luck and asked a girl named Wendy and to my complete surprise, she actually said yes! She even gave me a sweet kiss on the cheek, which I still count as my first real kiss. At that moment, I felt like the luckiest boy in the world. Of course, it wasn't really a romance but, instead, a sweet childhood moment that quickly faded away.

Those early crushes gave me little glimpses of belonging and being seen, feelings I carried with me into everything I did. One of the most significant places I felt that sense of connection was on stage.

I joined the Performing Arts Center for Children's musical version of *A Christmas Carol* at the Spreckels Theatre. I was cast as Tiny Tim, a role that felt like it was made for me. Celebrating diversity, the director had children of all races on stage, including me, a real disabled Tiny Tim who was determined to show the world what he could do.

I was described as a tough kid who never got frustrated or ran off the stage to his mom, but simply did what he was supposed to do. My mom shared with the paper that I carried emotional scars; I was still learning to heal. She even recalled a time at a presidential event at a mall when I saw Secret Service agents on the roof and started scream-ing in terror. It was a reminder that, behind my determination on stage, there was still a little boy working through deep fears.

When asked about my natural mom, I would simply say, "She never came back" and I'd move on with what I was doing. The article said you'd think all of this would have turned him into a real-life timid Tiny Tim, who was "bah, humbug" but, instead, was just the opposite.

I remember feeling a bit embarrassed when the script called for the Cratchit kids to help me put on my coat and hat because these were things I had always done for myself. I didn't want anyone to see me as helpless. Tiny Tim was known for being frail and sickly, but I was any-thing but that. I wanted everyone to see I was strong and didn't need help. My mom would proudly share that I could do fifty pushups, swim a dozen laps, and if I wanted to, I could beat any of the seventy-five other kids in the cast at arm wrestling. I was also a computer-game wiz-ard and could solve a Rubik's Cube in minutes. My mom always said, "Stefan is very strong-willed and determined to be as good as anybody else." That fierce determination wasn't just for show; it was something my parents had instilled in me from the very beginning.

That determination to show my strength wasn't just for the stage, it was something my parents nurtured every day at home for me to carry into my life. They believed in treating me just like everyone else, and they made sure I was never excluded or given an easy way out. They strengthened our character by giving us all chores, and I was no exception. I had to fold the weekly laundry for the entire family, sitting on the couch for hours with mountains of clothes piled beside me. If I wasn't folding, I was washing the dishes after family meals. And every day, I climbed up and down those stairs on my crutches, building not just physical strength, but resilience and independence that would carry me through life.

Another daily task my parents set for me was walking five blocks on my crutches, with my leg braces, to and from school each day. They knew it would build not only my physical strength but also my inner strength and resilience.

One day, I was especially excited because it was "prize day" at school. I had worked hard and earned a brand-new Yahtzee game for all that effort. But there was a problem: it was too big to fit in my backpack. So there I was, determined as ever, trying to juggle my crutch and the box in the same hand as I made my way home.

After a few shaky steps, I realized my hands were getting tired and it wasn't going to work. So, I did what any resourceful kid would do—I dropped the box on the ground and started kicking it with my crutch. I'd walk about ten feet on my crutches, then kick the box forward, and repeat.

Cars would slow down, and moms would roll down their windows to ask, "Do you need help, young man?" And every single time, I would proudly say, "No thank you, I've got it." I can only imagine what they thought, seeing a determined little boy crutch-walking and kicking a game box all the way home.

When I finally arrived, the box was torn to pieces. I didn't care because I knew I made it by myself. Looking back, I still don't know if it was pride, stubbornness, or just pure determination that kept me going. Or I wonder if I was more afraid of being seen as weak than I was of struggling.

Accepting help felt like surrendering something sacred, like my independence, my pride, maybe even my dignity. I had spent so long proving I could do it on my own, I didn't know how to let someone else carry part of the weight. In hindsight, my refusal wasn't just about the Yahtzee box, it was about a deeper fear that if I leaned too hard on anyone, I might fall. Maybe it was my pride that ruined that game, but I'd like to believe my perseverance proved that no matter how many obstacles were in my way (or how many kicks it took), I could get where I wanted to go and more importantly, I could do it all on my own.

That day with the Yahtzee box was more than a childhood memory; it was a glimpse of the determination my parents nurtured in me, a spirit that carried into every corner of my life.

Having a routine every morning gave me a sense of security, even though it was full of tasks I didn't always enjoy. Just getting dressed was a chore in itself. I had to put on my leg braces and then my body cast, like suiting up in body armor, a kind of bulletproof vest. I would even imagine that if anyone dared to hit me, they'd bounce right off. On some days, though, I skipped the armor and the braces altogether and used my wheelchair. Those were the mornings when I felt completely free, as if nothing could hold me back. Even with all that gear, both real and imagined, there were still constant reminders of what I couldn't do.

Living with a disability included all that. Even though I found comfort in my routine, I couldn't help but notice the things I missed out on. When we went on family vacations, I saw my brothers and sisters hike up to a waterfall while I had to wait in the water below. As beautiful as it was, I wished more than anything to climb with them. At beach camp, I'd drag myself from the sand to the water and back again, completely covered in sand. I got the full beach experience, but I was miserable doing it.

Still, even with those challenges, I was deeply grateful for our annual family vacations. They gave me a chance to be part of something bigger and create memories that I still cherish today. Some of the most special times were when we took our motorhome to camp or stayed at a beach house together. We also made trips with my grandparents to a cabin in the mountains, where I remember an amazing river that felt like a hidden treasure. I would walk alongside it with my crutches, soaking in the beauty around me. My parents made sure that I never missed out on a chance to experience the world around me.

Life seemed to be on the right track, but painful setbacks were waiting for me. I soon found out that the doctors needed to transplant my working thigh muscles into my abdomen. I had started struggling to cough up fluid, which led to dangerous buildup in my lungs. Knowing I would never walk again, the doctors decided to remove the working muscles from my legs to strengthen my core and help me breathe.

The pain that followed was like nothing I had ever felt. The transfer of muscles sent sharp, shooting pain down my right leg. I began enduring spinal taps, long needles piercing into my spine to inject pain medication. It was the most excruciating pain I could imagine. There I was, paralyzed, muscles removed from my legs, scars covering my body from my torso down, lying on my stomach as they pushed that needle in again and again. My mom would watch, cringing in helpless agony, knowing exactly how much I was suffering. She finally insisted to the doctors that there had to be a better way. Something permanent, so I wouldn't have to keep coming back to face that nightmare.

Eventually, they decided to make a long incision down my right side, go in, and cut the nerves to stop the pain for good. It was another battle in a childhood that felt like a never-ending series of trials, but through each one, God gave me the strength to keep going.

By then, my body carried a roadmap of scars: one on my lower left ankle joint, foot-long scars on both thighs, a scar across my stomach where they had implanted muscles, another beneath my left breast, and a long one stretching alongside my right torso. I couldn't feel anything in my right leg anymore.

I looked at my body, covered in scars, and felt a wave of something I couldn't quite name. Not shame—just…uncertainty. I remember lying there after one of the surgeries, staring at the ceiling, wondering what it was all supposed to mean. People said I was strong, that this would shape me. In those moments, I wasn't so sure. Hope felt distant, like a voice I used to hear more clearly. And maybe that was the hardest part, not the pain, but the quiet that followed it.

As a kid, I wondered who would ever love me like this. Who would see past the scars and accept me fully? I thought maybe, just maybe, I had finally faced enough pain for a lifetime. But as I finished those early years, from kindergarten to fifth grade, I realized my story was far from over. And so were my battles.

The biggest surgery, and the greatest test of my spirit, was still waiting for me.

LIFTED Value: **Foster Authenticity** Authentic leaders model vulnerability. Authenticity creates belonging and allows others to be fully themselves.

Lifted Insight:

"Accepting help felt like surrendering something sacred, like my independence, my pride, maybe even my dignity. I had spent so long proving I could do it on my own, I didn't know how to let someone else carry part of the weight."

Leadership Reflection: How do your own experiences of fear or vulnerability shape the way you lead and create space for others to be authentic?

CHAPTER 4

~

The Weight of Hope

A wave of terror ran through me as the doctor described yet another surgery so dangerous it was usually reserved for kids with spina bifida or severe scoliosis, and for those with a spinal curvature worse than forty degrees. He talked about fusing each vertebrae, starting at the base of my brain, as a permanent correction to my spine.

I sat motionless as the doctor revealed the details to us. He said he'd use metal plates, screws and rods to hold my spine together, hopefully healing as one bone in the end. I sobbed knowing I'd have to experience pain again. Hadn't I been through enough already? What would the recovery be like? I just started to fit in a little better at school. Now what?

I didn't understand. I thought that wearing my suit of armor each day was enough to correct it, but it wasn't. Apparently, I was still at risk of having more serious complications over time, like nerve pain, cardiovascular, or pulmonary issues that could cause difficulty breathing if it wasn't corrected now. While of course I didn't want those problems, I also didn't want to go through any more suffering.

The surgery came with many risks that were scary to me: blood clots, infection, and nerve damage. But the one that bothered me the most was when the doctor told us that I wouldn't be able to grow anymore. I was in the fifth-grade, around five-feet tall and of course I wanted to be taller. Why wouldn't they wait until after I went through puberty, where the biggest growth spurt takes place? I wanted to scream, "Let me grow as much as I can!" Nevertheless, I was set to undergo this surgery sooner rather than later. I couldn't help wondering if this was going to be one more reason why no one would want me?

After surgery, my growth stopped as expected. It was another blow to my self-esteem that I'd have to come to terms with. Even with this tough dose of reality, I was grateful that the nearly twelve-hour surgery was a success.

For some reason I thought I could catch my breath, having survived the worst part. But I quickly learned the hardest part was yet to come. I would be in a full body cast for most of my fifth-grade year.

I remember knowing that summer was passing while I lay there flat on my back, unable to move. The sunlight shifted across my ceiling day after day, each afternoon a longer, more agonizing stretch. I was bored, confined, and utterly lost in the endless ticking minutes, for how long I did not know. Then winter came, with Christmas and New Years passing by, and I was left wondering if I'd ever move again.

My family made sure I enjoyed Christmas by showering me with loads of presents. It was a momentary feeling of joy as I lay on my belly, in my full body cast, waiting for the next gift to open.

Quickly, I was returned to my bed where my body became stiff, full of pain, and itchy. Up until now my strength, resilience, and determination was enough to fill a large water well, but soon depression and sadness set in. I was left wondering if the well had run dry.

What if this is it? What if I stay like this—stuck, forgotten?

I tried to shake the thought, but it clung to me in the quiet. There was nothing I could do but distract myself by looking out the window, watching TV, or talking with whoever came by to check on me. My family was great, of course, but I could feel how uncomfortable my

Photo of Stefan at Christmas with his full body cast.
From Stefan Bean's personal photo library.

siblings felt. I looked like a paper doll that someone drew in a children's activity book, a sight they had never seen before. I'm sure they didn't know what to do or how to make me feel better. I look back now and wonder how a little child tolerated that? All I know is that I did.

But I didn't always feel strong. There were nights I lay awake in that cast and wondered if God had forgotten me. I tried to pray, but the words felt hollow. I told myself He had a purpose for my pain—but what kind of purpose leaves a child locked in his own body for months? The silence in the room began to mirror the silence I felt from God. And for the first time, I found myself questioning if He really was listening.

I believe it was my faith, however small or great, that gave me the unwavering hope and determination to bypass this hurdle. I was still here despite the many challenges I faced, which reinforced that God had a purpose for me, and that my life had never really been in danger. Like my experiences, I had faith that tomorrow would be better than today.

My imperfect faith pulled me through, along with an instinctive coping mechanism. After previous surgeries, I knew that I would fall asleep from the anesthesia and wake up when it was over. Every time I woke up, I felt relief, so before this surgery, I intentionally pictured how I would feel when it was over. To overcome the fear, I thought of images of happier times, like when I was a young child without a care in the world.

After picturing myself when surgery was over, I envisioned myself as fully recovered. This time it included getting my full body cast off, getting back to my normal routine at home with my family, and getting back to school.

I imagined hanging out with my friends and being just like everyone else. These were the images that kept me going. I instinctively went to this place of strength and created hope for myself. I never lost faith in the end story.

I found similarities in my coping strategy with Admiral Jim Stockdale's story of his own survival strategy as a prisoners-of-war hero, otherwise known as the Stockdale Paradox. Admiral Stockdale was imprisoned from 1965 to 1973 at the height of the Vietnam War. Much like my mindset, he would have unwavering faith in the endgame.

Stockdale's experiences were brutally different from mine, yet similar in fact that he never lost faith. He had to accept his reality of being tortured over twenty times during his imprisonment. He said, "I never lost faith in the end story. I knew I was going to get out, however I also never lost sight of what I was dealing with." When asked why he thought others didn't make it out, surprisingly he said, "The optimists were the ones who didn't make it out. They would set timeframes for getting out like telling themselves they'd be out by Easter. When that time passed and they were still imprisoned, they would move the date to Christmas. When that didn't happen over and over again, they ended up dying of a broken heart." (Collins, 2001, pp. 83-86).

I could never expect to understand the torture Admiral Stockdale endured, nor would I try to, but I was living in my own type of torture being unable to move. I felt checked out of life and it was really taking its toll on me. I had to dig deep for hope to continue.

I took what I learned from this experience into my role as a leader, where at times it seemed impossible to find hope. When you're leading a school that only has thirty percent of its population reading on grade level, you must confront and address that reality. But, you also need to have hope that your students will rise above it, too. The difficult part is figuring out how to encourage your teachers and students to also find that hope. I was able instinctively to see a positive future outside of my pain, but helping students to see this can be difficult.

In an article from *Inspire Engagement*, students were asked to close their eyes and create a vision of what their life would look like in five years and on into college. Then they were asked to see what life would look like in five years if they did not finish college. By doing this, students were directly connected to their future. Giving them tangible activities to learn this process is a great way to build it internally. Like my experiences, I had faith that tomorrow would be better than today (Staff writer, 2025)

This powerful activity is like transporting yourself into the moment. As a superintendent, to create a common vision for our schools, I've relied on this type of time machine activity with my teams, and clearly in my own life.

I was lucky I had some great teachers who were there for me while I lay flat on my back for nine months at home. I lost a lot of academic skills that weren't easy to attain in the first place. The gap widened, especially in my reading and writing skills. I was lucky to have a great fifth-grade teacher, Mr. Wetjen, a very calm and understanding man, who tried to support me the best way he could while I was home-bound. I remember he gave me lots of grace with assignments and grades, allowing me to turn in late work, creating simplified assignments, and offering encouragement.

Finally back at school, the hallway chatter felt like a foreign language. But slowly, words began to click. I joined some friends as they leaned against their lockers. My friend's laughter, once a distant echo, was now something I could join in on. School was still a minefield of challenges, but at least I wasn't navigating it alone.

Sixth-grade hit like a tidal wave. Suddenly, we were in middle school, trapped between the innocent curiosity of childhood and the baffling complexities of adolescence. Navigating the lunch table conversations was the worst; it felt impossible. Every new conversation was like a performance I wasn't prepared for. Most days I wanted to disappear.

Nothing would prepare me for the day Cara walked in. But there she was. She came from what seemed like nowhere; a bright comet that fell to the earth. She was a beautiful girl with the most arresting green eyes I'd ever seen. She was as nice as she was pretty. It only took one look from her to melt the hearts of every boy in the class, and I was no exception. My heart, that was usually locked in a vault of self-consciousness, felt like it was brought to life just by looking at her.

She was a heart stealer without even trying. My friend and I talked about her all the time. We spent hours dissecting her smile, her laugh, her every move. I never figured out how to tell her my feelings. So I waited, hoping to get the nerve.

The next thing I knew I saw them walking down the hall, hand in hand. She and *my friend* were a "thing." The world went silent. The weight in my gut was crushing. Didn't he know how I felt about her? I gushed over her daily. How could I miss the signs that they liked each other? Devastated beyond belief, I buried myself in homework, not just as a distraction, but because the alternative was worse, seeing them in the hallways was simply unbearable. Maybe I wasn't ready for love yet, but I knew even then that I wanted to be loved deeply someday—scars, crutches, and all.

When I returned to school, I was significantly behind academically. Having lost so many skills during fifth-grade, hiding it became an arduous task. I would cringe and my breath quickened every time my English teacher pulled out the reading comprehension cards. The last thing I wanted was for everyone to know that I still struggled to read and write.

Little did I know that when I stepped foot into Mr. Geisinger's class, he would change the trajectory of my life. There he was, the teacher who believed in me, sitting at his desk writing notes for the day's assignments. He was a Christian man who raised his family in faith. His kind smile and gentle demeanor were ever present, but his high expectations for his students were equally evident

He immediately recognized my strength: my "gift of gab." During his class I often interrupted him by goofing around and visiting with my friends. One day he pulled me aside and said, "Stefan, I don't really care that you're in a wheelchair, and that you're just learning English, and that you struggle to understand some of the assignments. I don't really care that you just returned from having a really big surgery. All I care about is that you become the best person you can be."

About that time, he assigned us a project: design and present a commercial for any product. I chose deodorant. When I rolled it onto my arm in front of the class, the stick flaked and crumbled right there in the case. Instead of panicking, I leaned into it and turned the moment into a parody. What could have been embarrassing became comedy gold. Mr. Geisinger and the whole class were cracking up—and honestly, so was I.

After class Mr. Geisinger pulled me aside and said, "Stefan, I know you struggle but you also have this gift. So from now on, I only want you to give oral presentations to the class. You don't have to read or take tests on reading comprehension; you just have to tell us about it."

I was happy about that. I knew I'd much rather be talking to the class, making people laugh, then doing reading comprehension packets and tests. Even though I was thinking I might be getting away with something, little did I know that Mr. G. had found a way for me to reach my potential at a time I didn't even see it all.

A few nerves never kept me from getting up in front of the class. What I didn't know was that my strength in conversational English would require me to use academic language, which improved greatly over time. It was confidence that made me feel like I was learning and progressing.

What I didn't know then, was that Mr. Geisinger changed the trajectory of my life. The power of one person allowed me to see my strengths and who I really was. This one person gave me confidence and the ability to see that my disability, my challenges, and my trauma did not define me. From then on, I started to get straight A's. Not only did Mr. G. give me the one opportunity that would change my life, but he would also give me *every* opportunity to be the best I could be.

I remember when we went to a sixth-grade camp in the mountains. I was prepared to accept my physical limitations for the activities I could do, much like when I vacationed with my family. The blue skies and beautiful terrain included lots of boulders and rocks. Our class was there to find the rocks that the Indigenous wrote on to communicate. I looked up and saw the mountain top as the other kids started their journey up the path. The pathway to the top was steep and high and I expected to be left at the bottom. To my surprise, Mr. G. allowed me to walk to the top of the mountain in my leg braces and on my crutches, just like the other kids. With my classmates surrounding me, we approached a boulder and they eagerly lifted me up.

Mr. Geisinger made me feel like I had a right to be there with those kids and to climb those boulders. It would have been easier for Mr. Geisinger to leave me at the bottom, but he wasn't about to do that. Mr. G. believed I could do it and I proved to myself that I could. That's the kind of teacher he was.

Finding a pathway around obstacles became automatic for me whenever I had to overcome pain, hurt, rejection, and more. My survival instincts were always there to carry me through difficult times. Many students don't recognize the pathways to move forward because no one taught them, encouraged them, or believed in them, like Mr. G. did for me. He saw my strengths and allowed me to use them in a way that made me shine. I felt success when I tapped into something that I did well.

We all need to find our greatness. If we don't know how to find it, it's like being stuck on an escalator unable to see the path forward and to latch onto hope. Mr. Geisinger instinctively knew what to do; he would find my strengths, build me up, and most importantly, he'd help me find it in myself. Now I had a path forward, a great path.

I was empowered and finally knew I belonged in this community. He gave me a sense of agency. I had a belief in my ability to succeed. And that's exactly what I was going to do. It only took one person's power to make me see me.

I would move on to conquer seventh and eighth grades. I continued receiving straight A's and building my confidence in my academic ability. This confidence transferred into my creative side when I sang a solo in the school play. Getting up in front of others helped me see myself as a leader. So I ran for class president and won. My speaking abilities and academic excellence would result in being chosen to give the Valedictorian speech to my class. It was like I finally found myself and I was successfully moving toward my future. The newspaper didn't hesitate to celebrate my accolades. They wrote an article about my speech and praised me for how far I had come in my journey.

I was able to deliver a speech to my classmates and during our church confirmation ceremony. My youth pastor, Mr. Christopher, heard my speech. It turns out that he was a delegate for the board for youth services, a Lutheran Church-Missouri Synod Board. Every three years, the board appointed speakers for the youth conference gathering in different cities. The conference held in 1985, had a patriotic theme and was hosted in Washington D.C. The conference would be titled *Faith, Freedom and Justice*. Mr. Christopher nominated me to be one of the three speakers, a very prestigious honor that I eagerly accepted.

The conference was a large gathering that brought together youth and adults from a variety of settings in their communities, congregations, and throughout the world. It was meant to impact the lives of many. Although I was anxious, this opportunity would affect me forever. I was able to speak words that would change lives.

The main purpose of my speech was to recognize and affirm the diversity of God's people, including the disabled. While there was a specific purpose of the conference, it was meant to celebrate the meaning of Christian joy in all life's situations, including during transitions and crisis, to which I could clearly attest.

The goal of my speech was to address justice for disabled people. I knew this was a once-in-a-lifetime opportunity to share something important on behalf of disabled people everywhere. This was the moment I could empower others through my own experiences as a disabled young man—and I had fifteen minutes to do it.

I wrote and prepared for this moment that was both exciting and overwhelming for a fourteen-year-old boy. But I knew I could do it. My dad and Mr. Christopher helped me write the speech. Mr. Christopher coached me to speak clearly and succinctly. My dad said, "Always start with a joke." So I planned to open with: "My dad told me to start with a joke and I said, 'Dad spare me and 15,000 other people.'" When I finally delivered it, that line got a big laugh—then I moved into my story and how I wanted to see disabled people treated.

I knew that I wanted my friends, including girls, to treat me with respect like everyone else. That's what I talked about that day.

I only allowed my dad to read my speech ahead of time because I wanted it to be fresh. I wanted to see if my speech had an impact on others now. I felt a slight nervousness but mostly excitement as I stepped on the stage. As I delivered the speech, a hush came over the crowd. I wasn't sure if that was good or bad, but I continued to speak from my heart. With sincere authenticity, I talked about how we're really just people like everyone else and we want them to know it's OK

Photo of Stefan at Faith, Freedom and Justice Conference, Washington D.C.
From Stefan Bean's personal photo library, 1985.

to approach us; we won't break. It's OK to be friends with us. We don't want to be treated any differently than anyone else.

I felt energized at that moment. I knew I was meant to be here to represent disabled people everywhere. I understood the importance of the moment. I knew I was their voice and I made sure to speak loudly and clearly.

As I finished my speech and exited the stage, the crowd roared. I could see my dad and Jordan and Cameron in the distance, waiting for me. Jordan and Cameron could care less, but my dad had a smile on his face and was beaming with pride. That's all I needed to see; I knew I did well. I walked off the stage, with leg braces and crutches, down the steps to my wheelchair. I sat down and rolled through the center aisle, heading towards my family.

I never expected what would happen next.....

LIFTED Value: **Transform Through Hope** Hope fuels resilience. Leaders who speak honestly about challenges while holding a vision for what can still be achieved help their teams endure. Hope keeps despair from having the final word.

Lifted Insight:

"I believe it was my faith, however small or great, that gave me the unwavering hope and determination to bypass this hurdle. I was still here despite the many challenges I faced, which reinforced that God had a purpose for me, and that my life had never really been in danger. Like my experiences, I had a belief that tomorrow would be better than today."

Leadership Reflection: When your team faces setbacks, how do you acknowledge the hardship while also holding out hope for the future?

CHAPTER 5

The Crowd Stands

Once my wheels hit the grass, the silence broke like a wave. The entire hillside exploded in cheers. Fifteen thousand people surged to their feet, each clapping, shouting, weeping. It was overwhelming. I looked up and saw a sea of faces, some blurry with tears, some smiling through them, all standing for me. The applause didn't just fill the air; it filled a space inside me I didn't know had been

> I wasn't surviving anymore. I was rising.

empty. For once, I wasn't the kid needing a lift, but now I was lifting others. That moment cracked something open. I wasn't surviving anymore. I was rising. I thought of every step I'd taken on crutches, every surgery scar, and every time I had felt invisible. And now... here I was. The boy no one saw, standing at the center of the world.

For a moment, I couldn't breathe. Not from nerves, not from fear, but from the weight of being seen. For the first time I was not pitied or just tolerated, I was *being celebrated*.

Unfamiliar people formed a crowd saying, "Amazing speech! Great job Stefan! Fantastic, young man!" A woman in a colorful scarf wiped a tear from her face. A young man covered in tattoos reached out to shake my hand. A boy in a wheelchair pumped his fist in the air as I rolled by.

As I moved towards my family, I caught sight of my dad and brothers cheering along with the crowd. There was a look of shock and disbelief in Jordan and Cameron's eyes—the kind only siblings can give—as if they were thinking, "OK...*that was something. What just happened?*" But even through their stunned expressions, I could tell they were proud of me. My dad stepped forward and said, "Great job, Stefan; I couldn't be more proud of you." Jordan and Cameron, finally out of their daze, gave me a nod—that quiet, unspoken kind of respect only brothers know how to give.

I was on a high coming back from Washington D.C. I felt like I was floating on a cloud, one that would never dissipate in the sky. This type of sheer elation was new for me and I liked it. So I bottled up this enormous amount of confidence and tucked it in my backpack for future use as I entered high school. That confidence didn't just shift how I saw myself—it started to shift how others saw me, too.

Like any freshman, I had the usual nerves about stepping onto a high school campus for the first time. But I also carried an excitement I hadn't felt before—like I belonged there in a new way.

It helped to see familiar faces. As I wheeled into the quad, packed with students reuniting after summer break, I spotted Eric and Tim at one of the lunch tables. Eric, who had been in Washington D.C. with me, smiled and called me over. He was poking his fingers through the holes in the table when he said, "Dude, that speech...you nailed it."

I laughed. "Yeah, thanks. It was pretty incredible."

We talked for a few minutes, catching up like old friends, before heading off to our first-period classes. It was the start of a new chapter in more ways than one.

After some small talk in class, the teacher began reviewing the syllabus when something unexpected happened. My name was called over the intercom. My stomach dropped. *I couldn't have possibly gotten into trouble already…Could I?* This never happened to me. It actually reminded me of Martin and the trouble he used to get into—*his* name was always being called.

I made my way to the front office, half-worried, half-curious. The principal, sharply dressed in a tailored gray suit with a red silk striped tie, greeted me with a smile. "Don't worry," he said. "You're not in trouble."

Then he got to the point: he'd heard about my speech in D.C., and thought I'd be the perfect person to speak at the upcoming kickoff assembly. I didn't hesitate. I said yes without blinking. As he continued to praise my ability to connect with people through my words, I felt a deep sense of pride rising up in me. It was the kind that came not from being noticed, but from being trusted to represent something bigger than myself.

In the weeks that followed, school settled into a steady rhythm. I got used to my schedule, figured out what each teacher expected, and, like most high school freshmen, couldn't help but notice all the beautiful girls on campus.

But soon it was time to step back into the spotlight. Kickoff assembly was approaching, and I knew exactly what I wanted to say. I decided to give the same speech I had delivered in Washington D.C.—the one that had moved thousands. Not because it was polished or impressive, but because it was *real*.

The day of the assembly arrived, and as I wheeled into the school auditorium, the nerves started to set in. The space was packed with classmates, teachers, upperclassmen I didn't know, and staff lined along the rows. I had spoken in front of thousands in Washington D.C., but this felt different. This was my own school, and these were my peers. I knew how quickly judgment could come in high school. Still, I took my place. With my crutches in hand and braces strapped on, I stood at the microphone and began.

I delivered the same speech I had given in Washington, about overcoming adversity, about resilience, about hope. But this time, something felt more personal. As I spoke, I looked into the crowd and saw faces I recognized—people who had seen me in the quad, in class, in passing. Some looked surprised. Others leaned forward. A few wiped tears.

When I finished, the auditorium erupted in applause, loud, powerful, and full of energy. I scanned the room and saw teachers smiling, students on their feet, and friends beaming with pride. This time, the size of the crowd didn't matter. What mattered was sharing my story with the people I walked or wheeled beside every day.

I knew that if they hadn't known me before, they knew me now. But it wasn't just me. I was proud to have spoken for the kids who rarely had a microphone, the ones so often hiding in plain sight. I spoke for the awkward, shy kid sitting alone. The one with glasses and braces, trying to disappear. The boy who never took off his hoodie, not because he was cold, but because he needed protection from a world that didn't understand him.

I spoke for the brilliant kid who couldn't survive in a system built for someone else's definition of "normal." For the girl who felt unattractive, unsure of how to even start a conversation. For the loud, boisterous bully who was looking for any kind of attention. And I spoke for the girl who only had one outfit to wear, washing it in the gym's washer every afternoon so she could show up clean the next day. Her reality never left survival mode.

My hope, then and now, was that the students who carried the appearance of being fine would start to look around. That they would see others. Stand up for others. *Be* the difference in someone's day. Because sometimes, it only takes one person noticing you to change your whole life.

Looking back, this was the moment when my compassion for marginalized students truly came into focus. After that assembly, something changed. People started approaching me. Not only the popular kids, but the quiet ones. The shy ones. The kids who purposely stayed invisible. I began noticing the subtle waves, the half-smiles, the soft eye contact from across the hall.

There was a quiet sense of connection beginning to bloom. I felt it as students nodded to each other in the hallway. Different kids from different crowds, seeing each other in a new light. And if I had played even a small part in creating that, in helping people feel seen, I knew I couldn't stop there. This wasn't just a speech. It was a calling.

That experience lit a spark, not just in others, but in me. After the assembly, what began as unintentional popularity gave me the confidence to run for freshman class president, and I won. I was thrilled. I finally had a platform to share my ideas, represent others, and, maybe most exciting of all, to speak and actually be listened to.

At the same time, something clicked academically. School started making more sense, which gave me the space to explore other parts of high school life—student government, sports, deeper friendships… and yes, the pursuit of a girlfriend. For the first time, I wasn't just surviving school; I was *thriving* in it.

Many of my friends played every sport I loved: football, basketball, and baseball. Eric, my best friend, played on the basketball team where he was coached by Mr. Heidtbrink, who also encouraged me to get involved in sports in other ways. So I joined as the team statistician, helping from the sidelines. But no matter how involved I was, feelings of sadness and inadequacy crept in every time I saw them play and remembered that I couldn't. It was another hurdle I had to clear, not physically but in my mind.

I'd watch them race down the court, leap into high-fives, and slam their bodies into one another in celebration after a big play. I wanted so badly to be part of that, to *feel* that connection. More than the movement, I longed for the bond that came with it—the way they connected through the rhythm of the game. I often wondered if they knew how lucky they were to do something so many take for granted.

I did get the chance to play in some wheelchair games at a recreation center off campus. And as much as I enjoyed competing, it still didn't connect me to my friends, the guys I saw every day at school. So I found another way in. I started out as a scorekeeper, then became a statistician, and eventually team manager for the teams my friends played on. That role gave me a front-row seat to the action. More importantly, it gave me access to the camaraderie I had been craving.

I had a blast riding the team buses to games, soaking in the energy. We'd joke, sing, shout—all the stuff guys did back then to pump each other up before tip-off. I wasn't on the court, but I was in it: in the brotherhood, in the moments, in the team.

Eric and I often hung out with Tim until he transferred to another school. That same freshman year, two new friendships began to take shape: Laurie and Enrique. Laurie had a quiet warmth to her, and Enrique was the funniest person I had ever met. We all connected quickly, but it didn't take long for me to realize that my feelings for Laurie went deeper than friendship.

Eric was dating Kari back then so he was busy. Soon after, Enrique fell for Laurie. What no one knew, not even Laurie, was that I had fallen for her, too. Laurie was kind, funny, and had this inviting, connecting smile that made you feel like you mattered. She was the first girl who truly made me laugh. The kind of laugh that felt effortless and safe. And somehow, she made me feel truly seen. We'd talk about everything—school, life, faith. She gave me her full attention in a way that made my heart quietly, stubbornly, hope for more.

My brother would later tease me, saying he used to hear me in the bathroom, practicing conversations with Laurie in the mirror. Apparently, I was rehearsing what I'd say, how I'd say it, maybe even how I'd smile when I said it. He thought it was hilarious. I thought it was preparation.

But all that preparation came crashing down one day. I turned a corner on my way to class, and there they were—Laurie and Enrique kissing! It was like watching a shocking scene from a movie that made everyone in the audience gasp. The new love of my life was gone before I ever had her.

That should've been me. Didn't she see me? Didn't I matter?

I looked away, pretending I hadn't seen anything, but I had. And I wouldn't forget it. I was devastated and I cried for what felt like months. And the hurt this time was way more intense then with Cara. This one split my heart in two. I thought I had built up enough strength to handle heartbreak, but nothing prepared me for the ache of never even getting the chance. It wasn't jealousy. It was invisibility. Again. The kind that makes you wonder if you'll ever be the one someone chooses. But as time passed and the ache dulled, Laurie and I did find our way back to a real friendship, even though something *lingered*.

It was a deep pain of a certain kind that I had never felt before, and this time, it would take a while to heal. My heart eventually mended, but my mind kept circling the same question: *Why did all my friends have girlfriends and I didn't?*

I didn't fully recognize it yet, but a pattern was beginning to take shape: meaningful friendships with girls who confided in me, trusted me, and cared for me deeply, though not in the way I had hoped. It was confusing at times, but also, in its own way, comforting. And it would shape how I approached relationships, trust, and love going forward.

The following year, our school moved to a new campus. I missed the comfort of the old one, with the shade from the green trees and the quad where we all used to gather between classes. The new campus didn't have that same feeling. With its two-story buildings and a single, steep staircase, it felt more like a fortress, even a little prison-like, especially for someone like me. My classes were upstairs, and without an elevator, my only option was to climb. So every day, I gripped my crutches and tackled that staircase. I always made it, but by the time I reached the top, my arms were burning and my body aching. Still, I pushed through. I always did.

One day, when I came to school in my wheelchair, I was floored when my friends stepped to each side of me and lifted me up the stairs, chatting casually the whole way as if it were nothing. I felt this warmth in my chest because I knew they weren't doing it out of obligation. They did it because they wanted to help their friend.

From that day on, whenever I showed up in my wheelchair, it became routine. Different friends would jump in without hesitation. It was just something they did. Not because they had to; because I mattered to them. And that meant everything to me.

That simple act of being carried up those stairs became more than just a daily routine. It became a metaphor I carried with me my entire life. Sometimes, we all need people to come alongside us, to help lift us when we can't make it on our own. That lesson shaped how I saw leadership, friendship, and faith. And it reminded me that strength isn't always about walking alone; sometimes, it's about letting others walk with you.

But not all moments of inclusion were so symbolic or serious. Some were loud, sweaty, chaotic, and filled with laughter.

My brothers were amazed at my upper body strength back in the day. Both of them, athletes through and through, would grab me and wrestle me to the ground. They were always shocked when I held my own against them. They never went easy on me, and it was just as well. Honestly, they would've regretted it if they had.

At school, Eric would sometimes steal my crutches just to mess with me. He'd return them eventually but never too quickly. Even though I acted like I was annoyed, I secretly loved it. There was some-thing about being treated like *every other guy* that meant everything to me. Nothing said "you're one of us" quite like being pulled into the noise and the nonsense of brotherhood.

By the end of high school, more girls had come into my life. They made me feel special, but in the end, they remained just friends. Although I was grateful for those friendships, I was very lonely. Deep down, I craved more. I started to wonder if something was wrong with me. I was always the friend, the safe choice, the one girls confided in but never the one they chose. Was it the wheelchair? The scars? My skinny legs? Or was I just fundamentally unlovable? These weren't just fleeting thoughts—they followed me into every interaction. I smiled and laughed, but underneath, I was carrying a quiet ache that whispered: maybe you're the kind of guy people respect… but never love.

Prom was a beautiful night. I went with a close friend, and for a moment it felt like something out of a dream. We danced to "Two Hearts" by Phil Collins, shared an elegant dinner, and laughed among friends beneath the soft glow of tropical lights. She looked stunning, and the evening was unforgettable in its own way. But as beautiful as she was, I knew in my heart she wasn't mine. Still, I believed that one day, the right person would come, and that God was saving something special for me. And while that deeper connection hadn't come yet, my life was still rich and full.

High school was an amazing time in my life. Spending time with friends, being part of the sports community, and finding my place in the rhythm of school kept me grounded and happy. There were a few moments of connection here and there, but nothing ever turned into a lasting relationship. Still, I held on to the quiet hope that love would come in its own time. Looking back, I can see that some things are meant to unfold slowly, and that waiting often teaches us more than rushing ever could.

Windy and I had a friendly rivalry throughout high school. We were both high achievers, competing for top honors. In eighth grade, I was chosen as Valedictorian, and while she congratulated me, I could tell she had hoped it would be her. By senior year, it was her turn. A B plus in AP English knocked me out of the running, and I had to accept that I would not be giving the final speech. It was a humbling moment, but it taught me how to handle disappointment with grace. In the end, Windy delivered a beautiful speech, and we were both named

"Most Likely to Succeed" in the yearbook, a recognition that still meant a great deal to me.

I had the drive to make that happen, yet my direction in becoming a leader would begin with different interests that would ultimately guide me to leading others. My interest in science initially steered me towards becoming a doctor. However, I quickly realized that I wanted to be a businessman like Alex P. Keaton on the hit show *Family Ties*. I saw myself in him as a confident young man with dynamic energy and drive. He was an intelligent innovator, who was always thinking outside the box, like I was. So I started carrying around a briefcase just like he did. I no longer wanted to be a doctor. I decided to become a businessman.

A childhood friend and influential businessman would mentor me further. Bill Sanderson was a young college student when he, and a bunch of guys, moved into a house by the Beans. I was just a small boy when my mom and I greeted him at the front door of their house. Bill was surprised to see my mom holding me with one arm with an apple pie in her hand. No one on the block was keen on having a group of college boys in the neighborhood, but in hindsight, building a relationship with Bill was probably a good move on mom's part. If they threw parties, we didn't know it. They actually proved to be good neighbors.

I learned later that Bill would go on to open Popcorn Palace in malls across Southern California and become a very successful businessman and philanthropist. I never lost sight of Alex P. Keeton, but I knew Bill Sanderson was the real thing. He became my mentor who would show me the ins-and-outs of business. He encouraged me to join every business group I could on campus, and I did. I'd converse with different groups of my peers and learn about business practices. Bill told me USC had a very strong entrepreneurship program and I should apply. I was able to receive grants and scholarships to USC, my first choice. It was an easy decision, so I was on my way.

My dad took me to USC. My heart pounded with excitement and fear. My dad was quiet. When we drove through the streets of Los Angeles, for the first time, I noticed the number of homeless on the streets, who were surrounded by colorful graffitied walls. Their plight struck a deep feeling of sadness within me. Here I was lifted up by so many people throughout my life, who made it possible for me to be going to one of the most prestigious colleges around. And here they were, the mentally ill, or those who had succumbed to addiction. To be on the streets, they must have used up everyone who tried to help. Or worse, maybe they had nobody in the first place. I felt fortunate to have so many influential people in my life who helped carry me through.

My dad pulled up to Philippes, a historic deli, established in 1908, in Los Angeles, that was known for its signature French dip sandwiches. My dad and I enjoyed our lunch, making small talk about my new journey to come. My mom was home with the kids and had tearfully said goodbye. I know she believed in me, but she had cared for me through so many trials and tribulations it had to be hard for her to let me go. My dad was the strong one who could handle the extended goodbye.

When we arrived at USC, it was just as beautiful as I remembered it was when we had taken our high school tour. The USC band was playing and the school songs invoked a sense of pride instantly. I was full from eating at Philippes, but I remember the smell of Carl's Jr. that was centered right in the middle of the campus, a smell and taste I would enjoy for many years to come.

Many students were being dropped off to move into their dorms. The traffic was slightly backed up as they unloaded boxes, tables, pillows, and lamps. I looked over and noticed a tall, white freshmen dorm that would become my new home. My dad carried some of my belongings as I sat a box on my lap and we approached my new room. The Resident Assistant approached us to say hi. He had a visor on and was friendly, offering any help that I needed. My dad and I placed the last of my things on the bed. The time had come for him to leave. He hugged me and said goodbye. I felt emotion well up inside of me. And then my dad–the strong, silent, tough one–started to cry.

LIFTED Value: **Empower Through Strength** Empowerment comes when leaders entrust others with meaningful responsibility. Delegating is not just about getting things done; it is about showing people you believe in their capacity. When leaders empower, they multiply strength in the organization.

Lifted Insight:

"*The applause didn't just fill the air; it filled a space inside me I didn't know had been empty. For once, I wasn't the kid needing a lift, but now I was lifting others. That moment cracked something open. I wasn't surviving anymore. I was rising.*"

Leadership Reflection: When have you experienced empowerment that shifted how you saw yourself?

CHAPTER 6

Fire and Formation

My dad wiped the tears from his face as he gave me a quick, tight hug and whispered goodbye. It was the first time I had ever seen him cry. This was the same man I had always known as steady, stoic, the disciplinarian in our house, the one who set the rules and made sure they were followed. There was never a question of his love, but he reserved emotion for rare occasions. That part was my mother's domain; her tears arrived often especially when a new child entered our family and sorrowful ones when one left. But my dad, standing there, openly sobbing? That was something I had never witnessed.

His tears caught me completely off guard, and for a moment, I didn't know how to respond. The puzzled look on my face probably said everything. I had assumed he'd feel a quiet relief: one more kid launched, one less mouth to feed, one more room freed up in a busy household. But instead, his emotion revealed something deeper. This goodbye wasn't a logistical milestone. It was a heartfelt, bittersweet letting go.

My parents had poured so much into raising me, years of effort, sacrifice, and steadfast love, that I assumed sending me off to a prestigious university would feel like a celebratory culmination. And in many ways, it was. But later, my mom confided that this was the hardest goodbye she had ever experienced. Even though they believed in me, and knew they had given me the tools to face the world, I now realize how daunting it must have been to release their son, especially a son with unique challenges, into the unknown. They weren't just proud; they were also heartbroken.

As I left my dorm room to grab dinner, a tingling spread through my body. I couldn't tell if it was excitement or fear; probably both. For the first time in my life, I felt truly alone. No Beans to lift me up. No protective cocoon of family to catch me if I fell. This time, it was just me, navigating a brand-new world on my own.

> For the first time in my life, I felt truly alone. No Beans to lift me up.

With each turn of my wheels toward the dining hall, a quiet doubt crept in. Had the independence I practiced at home prepared me for the real thing? Was I truly ready to manage this on my own, without my family's constant safety net? For a fleeting moment, I was transported back to the same knot-in-the-stomach feeling I had on my first day of elementary school, that raw mix of loneliness and fear when everything felt unfamiliar and overwhelming.

But loneliness did not last long. As I entered the lobby, a brunette with a big, welcoming smile and striking green eyes turned to me and said, "Let's go to dinner." I was stunned, and incredibly relieved. She had no idea how much her simple invitation meant to me at that moment. Her name was Kim Estock, and as we walked off toward the freshman dining hall, I had no idea I was stepping into the beginning of a beautiful friendship.

As we approached the food line, I couldn't help but silently mouth the word, "*What?!*" It felt like I had just entered a dream. For years, my mom's homemade dinners had filled our table with love and flavor. But this was a whole new universe. Burgers, fries, grilled chicken, steaming soups, loaded salad bars, pizza, pasta, vegetables, desserts were all for my choosing. The options seemed endless. I felt like a kid walking into a candy store, grinning with the realization: *I get to do this every day?*

Kim and I found a table, and soon a few other students joined us. One of them was Wendy Wilson, whose dark, wavy hair bounced as she spoke with an energy that immediately lit up the space. Her laugh was contagious, the kind that made you laugh even if you missed the joke. We took turns sharing where we were from, what we planned to study, and how we hoped to get involved on campus. When it was my turn, I spoke with passion about my dream of becoming a business owner. To my surprise and delight, they listened intently and cheered me on, affirming that I belonged in this new world.

At that moment, something shifted. I no longer felt like an outsider trying to find his place; I felt like I belonged. Surrounded by new faces and unexpected kindness, I knew deep down that I was going to be okay.

It didn't take long before I was well on my way to gaining the infamous freshman ten pounds. With four meals a day including breakfast, lunch, dinner, and a midnight snack, the dining hall became more than a place to eat; it became our social hub. That first year was unlike any other. I met new people constantly and cultivated friendships that stretched across every corner of campus life. While I had plenty of male friends, I found myself naturally connecting with women. Maybe it was because I was raised by such a nurturing, empathetic mother, someone who saved me in every sense. That influence had quietly shaped how I related to others.

Over dinner, my new friends told me about the Lyon Center, the campus recreational sports complex. After we ate, we decided to check it out. I was astonished. The facility spanned 80,000 square feet and buzzed with energy. Wendy, who had just started working there and was clearly athletic, described it as the heartbeat of student life, a place where people didn't just work out but gathered, relaxed, and connected. It immediately felt like somewhere I wanted to spend time.

Inside, the facility featured expansive courts for basketball, volleyball, and racquetball, along with an impressive array of cross-training equipment. Whether I was working out solo or with friends, I knew this place would quickly become part of my routine.

The very next morning I went to Lyon Center for a workout. While chatting with a few students at the front desk, I found out they were hiring. Without hesitation, I applied. To my surprise and excitement, I was offered a position right there at the front desk. At the time, I figured it was just a job to help pay the bills and meet people. I had no idea how important this place would become in my story.

Eventually, I moved from the front desk to the weight room, where my job was to re-rack the 45-pound weights students left scattered across the floor. It was a humbling and oddly empowering experience. Me, a kid in a wheelchair, bending down, hoisting weights, and wheeling them across the room to put them back where they belonged.

The Lyon Center quickly became more than work. It was a hub of student life, and I loved being in the middle of it. Every shift felt like a mini networking event. I met dozens of students each day, many of whom became familiar faces. Over time, casual chats turned into real relationships. One of those connections, though I didn't know it then, would come to mean more to me than I ever could have imagined.

USC pride pulsed through the Lyon Center. You could feel it in the conversations, the gear, the energy. I loved being part of that culture. Everywhere I went on campus, I felt like I belonged. It wasn't the home I had grown up in. But it was becoming my home, filled with pride, camaraderie, and connection. As the semester rolled on, so did football season. Between classes, workouts, and shifts at work, I'd meet my new friends at the games, swept up in the roar of the crowd and the rhythm of college life.

I'd hear the marching band echo across campus during practice, their drums pounding like a heartbeat. In the distance, the sharp grunts of the football team during drills added to the constant rhythm of campus life, a rhythm that was alive and unforgettable. Those sounds weren't just background noise; they were the soundtrack to my transformation. With every beat, I felt more connected to the Trojan spirit. That pride embedded itself so deeply in me that even now, years later, whenever I return to campus, those same echoes bring it all rushing back—reminding me not just where I studied, but where I truly found myself.

At first, I thought I could get around campus with just my crutches, but it didn't take long to realize that USC was far bigger and more spread out than I had imagined. The daily treks between classes wore me down, and I knew I needed a better way. So I switched to my wheelchair full-time. Thankfully, it was brand new and smooth, making it easy to glide from one end of campus to the other. What started as a practical adjustment quickly became a symbol of freedom. I wasn't limited; I was moving with purpose.

Before I left for college, my parents ordered me a new wheelchair. I had requested a neon pink one. I thought it would be bold and fun. But when the first chair arrived, it was more Pepto-Bismol than neon. My parents took one look and said, "We're sending it back," and I didn't argue. A few months later, the real neon pink chair showed up, and this time, it was perfect. There was something about that color that made it loud, unapologetic, and distinct. I loved it immediately. What I didn't realize at the time was how much it would draw people in. That chair wouldn't just carry me across campus, it would make me visible, memorable, and unexpectedly approachable.

In my new pink wheelchair, I quickly became a fixture on campus, zipping through the main walkway between classes, passing familiar faces who'd call out, "Hey Stefan!" Once I gave up the crutches, it felt like I had transformed into an express train, on a schedule, skipping

Photo of Stefan with friends, in his pink wheelchair.
From Stefan Bean's personal photo library.

stops, moving with purpose. Jeff, more of a slow-and-steady guy, would wave as I flew past and joke, "I'll catch the next one!"

Over time, my popularity grew. Not because I was trying to be noticed, but because I was always connecting. What started as simple daily interactions became a wide network of friends and acquaintances. Some said I was smooth, others joked I should major in networking, but for me, it was never calculated. I've always genuinely loved talking with people, smiling, making them feel seen. My route through the center of campus wasn't just the fastest way to class, it was my stage, my social lane, and my confirmation that I belonged.

The Lyon Center, though, felt routine and just another regular afternoon....until *she* walked in. A young woman with dark hair and a quiet confidence showed up for the shift, and we were paired together to re-rack weights. At first, I couldn't help but think, *She's kind of tiny. I hope she can handle the heavier plates.* But within moments, she had me rethinking everything. She lifted with ease, moving through the room like she belonged there. Turns out, she was incredibly fit and worked out regularly. I stood corrected and intrigued. There was something about her I couldn't quite name at the time, but it stayed with me.

Every shift we worked together, we talked effortlessly. There was a calm steadiness to her, something grounding, like she carried a quiet wisdom well beyond her years. Bit by bit, her story unfolded. She had grown up in Lemoore, a small farm town outside Hanford in Kings County. Her parents were immigrants from Portugal, and she was raised in a modest house, helping on the family farm. There was no sense of pretense, only gratitude, humility, and strength. The more I learned about her, the clearer it became. My initial curiosity was quickly blossoming into profound respect.

We talked about everything from music and movies to politics, where things really got interesting. She didn't just listen, she challenged. I'd bring what I thought was a solid argument to the table, and she'd dismantle it with a calm, confident smile, like she'd been waiting for me to take the bait. We debated with bold opinions, stubborn persistence, and just enough humor to keep it playful. Somehow, by the end of every conversation, we'd both shifted, each giving a little ground without ever admitting it. She was the first person in a long time who truly pushed me to think differently. I wasn't quite sure what that meant yet, but it stuck with me.

Her name was Janet. At the time, she was just a co-worker, a sparring partner in debate, a strong woman with a quiet presence. Something about her lingered with me longer than most.

In my spare time, I poured myself into working out at the Lyon Center. My upper body grew stronger by the week—lifting, pushing, pulling—I could feel the transformation. But underneath that physical progress was a quieter concern. After my last surgery, my doctor had warned me about Post-Polio Syndrome (PPS) which is a neurological disorder that can resurface decades after the initial infection, often without warning. I didn't want to be one of them. I wasn't just building muscle, I was trying to outrun a debilitating future.

The possibility of developing PPS lingered in the back of my mind. It could mean muscle weakness, loss of upper body strength, even fatigue that could sideline the independence I'd fought so hard to build. I often wondered if that strength slipped away, who would I become without it? That's why the gym wasn't optional. It was a kind of insurance policy, a way to fight back against a potential future I feared more than anything.

Back in grade school, I had met a para-athlete who had once competed on the world stage. I'd mentioned him before. His story stayed with me for years. But now, at USC, his influence has resurfaced another way. His physical ability no longer inspired me; I was inspired by his mindset. He didn't just overcome his disability, he *owned* it. That's what I carried with me during every workout: the belief that I could do more than survive. I could lead, inspire, and thrive.

Up until college, the Olympian had been the only person with a disability I truly connected with, someone who understood my world without needing it explained. I was confident, yes, but I always felt a subtle divide between me and those who moved through life without physical limitations. My challenges were different. My path, steeper. That sense of being "apart" followed me until I met Garrett.

Garrett lived on the first floor of our dorm. Like me, he used a wheelchair. He had Cerebral Palsy, which meant mobility was a constant challenge, and communication could be, too. But in our daily conversations, I never noticed a single barrier. He spoke with thoughtfulness and wit, and I found myself genuinely enjoying our talks. More than that, he gave me something I hadn't expected: a quiet reassurance. Just by showing up each day handling classes, campus life, and his independence, Garrett reminded me that *we* belonged here. We didn't have to prove it. We already did.

That same year, I met Sean, another paraplegic student on campus. When I found out he had a wife, I was stunned—in the best way. I had never seen that before, someone like me, building a life with someone who loved them deeply. As he spoke about her, his face lit up with tenderness, and my heart followed. He wasn't just surviving; he was thriving. For the first time, I allowed myself to picture it, too. A future filled with love, companionship, laughter in the kitchen, and the kind of everyday partnership I'd always dreamed about.

And then there she was: Shannon. Tall, athletic, confident. A former high school cheerleader from Mission Viejo, with rich brown hair and deep, observant eyes. She walked with ease, laughed loudly, and carried herself like she knew exactly who she was. Compared to the slow, steady connection I'd been building with Janet, Shannon felt like a spark. She was fast, bright, and hard to ignore.

We met in the freshman dorms and quickly formed a friendship. She was more worldly, more experienced. She taught me things, showed me parts of life I hadn't yet explored. We started sharing meals, studying late into the night at the library. There was chemistry, no doubt about it. And yet, something in me hesitated, but I ignored it. I didn't want to overthink it. I just wanted to fall.

Shannon and I started spending time at the top of Doheny Memorial Library, deep in the stacks which were USC's quietest corners, where rows of books created hidden alcoves and pockets of privacy. It was a place serious students escaped to when they didn't want to be found, where whispered conversations and rustling pages replaced the noise of campus life. It felt like our own secret world which tucked away between the shelves, removed from everything else. I wasn't sure if we were there to study or be near each other. Maybe both. But I knew something was building.

I'd be lying if I said I didn't have an ulterior motive when I brought Shannon up to the stacks that day. The silence was thick, broken only by the occasional rustle of paper or the soft creak of a chair. The smell of old books, the warmth of filtered light—it all made the moment feel suspended in time. I turned toward her, heart pounding, and with every ounce of courage I had, I leaned in and kissed her. She kissed me back. It was gentle, electric, somehow surprising and expected.

From that moment on, we were inseparable, studying side by side, walking across campus, sharing meals and stolen glances. Our emotional connection deepened, and soon, so did the physical one. I started falling for her, quickly.

When Thanksgiving break came and we went home to our families, I missed her more than I expected. She missed me, too. That time apart created a kind of hunger. We were rushing toward something neither of us fully understood.

When we returned from break, a quiet pride swelled in my chest. I had a real girlfriend. Not just someone to study with or flirt across the dining hall, but someone who chose me, fully. It felt like I had finally found her, the one who saw me, wanted me, and wasn't afraid to show it. I brought her home to meet my high school friends, and we went to the homecoming game together, dancing under the lights like we were writing a new chapter. Everything felt solid on the outside. But beneath the surface, something small and unnamed had started to stir.

This felt like my first *real* relationship. Shannon didn't just understand how I felt—she returned those feelings, openly and without hesitation. It made me reevaluate everything that came before: Cara and Laurie...those were infatuations. This felt different. Like two lives finally moving in the same direction.

After the holidays, I came back to campus eager to pick up where we left off. I had built my routine around her, woven her into my days without even realizing it. She was in the walks between classes, the late-night study sessions, the imagined future. I couldn't picture life without her. And then—she showed up with someone else.

No call. No conversation. Just her, walking through campus holding hands with another guy. Like I had never existed. Her head stayed down, avoiding my eyes, as if I were a ghost in the life we once shared. What stunned me wasn't just that she had moved on, it was that she had done so mid-sentence, in the middle of our story.

I found myself avoiding the very places that once felt like ours; the dining hall, the library, even the quad. I couldn't bear to see them together. Couldn't comprehend how something so full of life could be gone and cease to exist. It felt like our six-months had been erased in one careless edit and along with it, a piece of my heart.

My mind played the same loop over and over, like a scratched record stuck in rewind. First, I relived the good moments, only to question whether they were real at all. Then came the second-guessing: *Were there signs I missed when she met my friends or at homecoming? Did she start drifting before I noticed?* A darker question sometimes crept in: *What if Shannon, like the bully back in elementary school, just couldn't accept me for who I was?* I obsessed over the timeline. *Who was this guy? Why him, not me?* The only theory that made sense was that she was influenced. Maybe her new sorority sisters nudged her in another direction.

Eventually, the grueling cycle burned. I stopped asking questions I'd never get answers to. Still, one thought lingered like a whisper I didn't want to hear: *Was it even real? Or was I the only one who thought it was?*

Looking back, I can see it more clearly, but that took time. A lot of time. The heartbreak didn't immediately feel like a lesson; it felt like a failure. That relationship, however flawed, had shown me something I hadn't fully believed before that I could be loved, wanted, pursued. That I could share my life with someone. Shannon wasn't the one, but she was part of the journey. And somewhere beyond the ache, I began to believe the right one was still out there, waiting to be revealed.

At the start of my sophomore year, I was still quietly nursing the wounds from the breakup with Shannon. Emotionally bruised and trying to reset, I threw myself into one of the toughest classes on campus: *Bible as Literature*. Until then, I had always felt at home in academia. But this class rattled me. I turned in my first major paper with confidence—and got back a D. I remember staring at the grade in disbelief, my ego bruised and my confidence shaken.

As I sat there trying to process it, a tall, energetic blond guy from the back of the room walked over and plopped down next to me. "Rough day?" he asked with a grin. We started talking about the class, about being raised Lutheran, about how ridiculously difficult the professor was. He was easy to talk to, naturally outgoing, and before I knew it, we were cracking jokes and swapping stories. "Let's hang out," he said casually. So we did.

We headed to the Lyon Center, and that afternoon turned into the start of a friendship that would shape the rest of my life. His name was Mark Schmidt. He saw me—really saw me—not as the guy in the wheelchair, but as someone worth knowing. We clicked instantly. His energy, humor, and lack of hesitation made him feel like the brother I didn't know I needed. I didn't realize it at the time, but meeting Mark wasn't just a bright spot in a hard season. It was the beginning of a lifelong bond that would carry into some of my biggest future chapters.

Sophomore year felt worlds away from the connection and spontaneity of freshman dorm life. I had moved off campus, and with that came an unexpected sense of isolation. Gone were the casual run-ins, shared meals, and late-night laughs in the hallway. Socializing now required effort, and I found myself missing the ease of those early friendships. The lingering ache from my breakup with Shannon didn't help. I was searching for something to fill the quiet.

That's when I decided to try something new: I joined the Trojan Knights, USC's historic spirit and service organization rooted in brotherhood, service, and Trojan pride. The group was known for guarding the Victory Bell, supporting athletic traditions, and building community through service. It offered me a structured connection, something I desperately needed. Whether I was volunteering at events, helping with campus traditions, or standing on the sidelines during football games, I found myself re-engaging, not just with campus, but with myself.

While the Trojan Knights gave me a sense of structure and pride, my friendship with Mark offered something else entirely: laughter, energy, and a reminder that college was also supposed to be fun. By junior year, our bond had only become stronger. So when we were invited to help re-establish Phi Kappa Alpha, a fraternity returning to campus after losing its charter, we both jumped at the chance.

Mark and I joined Pi Kappa Alpha with a small group of guys who, like us, wanted to build something meaningful. Many would go on to be incredibly successful—movie producers, entrepreneurs, even venture capitalists. By the end of junior year, we had secured a house on the row, surrounded by the legacy fraternities with their columns, traditions, and weekend parties.

Our house became a hub of activity with loud music, laughter spilling out onto the porch, the energy of college life in full swing. While the others drank and partied hard, I was there for something different. I didn't drink much, but I didn't need to. I loved the vibe, the camaraderie, and the chance to connect with people. Being surrounded by such social electricity lit me up. It reminded me that inclusion wasn't conforming, it was about showing up fully as yourself.

It wasn't about parties or social status. It was building something from scratch. We weren't joining a fraternity with a long list of traditions. We were shaping its future. This leadership opportunity lit a fire in both of us. Creating a new culture. Forming our own brotherhood. Carving out a place for ourselves on the row. And doing it alongside Mark made it even better. He never treated me differently. Never hesitated to loop me in. Always pushed me to be myself. Together, we weren't just joining something. We were building it.

Being a founding father of Pi Kappa Alpha wasn't just a title. It was a responsibility. There was no blueprint. No established rituals. No older brothers to guide us. We were the ones creating the culture, setting the tone, deciding what kind of men we wanted to be. I leaned into leadership naturally. I facilitated discussions, organized events, managed logistics, and helped shape a vision for who we were becoming. It wasn't easy. We disagreed. We failed. We regrouped. We tried again. But in the process, I learned how to listen, how to build consensus, how to lead through influence rather than authority. These weren't fraternity lessons. They were life lessons. And they would serve me in ways I couldn't yet imagine.

My friendship with Mark quickly rivaled the bond I'd once had with Eric, my closest friend in high school. When Eric left for San Diego State and I came to USC, we naturally drifted apart as life got busy and our worlds diverged. But Mark filled that space in a way I didn't even know I needed. Like Eric, he never saw the wheelchair. He just saw me. And maybe more importantly, he treated me like any other guy, with zero hesitation and full throttle.

Mark and I did wild, reckless things that probably made onlookers think we'd lost our minds. One of our favorite stunts was getting from our apartment to campus by turning my wheelchair into a two-man vehicle. I'd grab onto the back of his bike, and he'd take off, pulling me like a chariot through the streets of USC. Right before class, I'd let go and slingshot myself straight into the building, grinning like a maniac.

But Mark wasn't just wild, he was fearless. And sometimes, that meant I had to be fearless, too, whether I liked it or not. Eric had always been careful not to push me too far. Mark…not so much. He'd fly down the hall with me at full speed and yell right before letting go so I could steer into an open door. Once, he forgot to warn me, and I crashed headfirst into the drywall, leaving a dent shaped like my head, body, and wheelchair.

I probably should have been mad. But instead, I laughed. Hard. Because for all the chaos, Mark reminded me of something vital: that I didn't have to be careful to be included. I could be part of the madness too.

I'm not sure why I let Mark do it again, but I did. This time, I was smarter, or so I thought. I didn't trust him to warn me, so I planned my own defense: hands up, face protected, ready to brace for impact. He pushed. I waited for the shout, hoping, maybe even needing, to hear some sign that he cared about my safety. But nothing. Just silence. And then, as fate would have it, three girls walked into the hallway right as I slammed on my brakes. My hands, gripping tightly to my wheels, caused my chair to tip, and I went tumbling to the ground in dramatic slow motion. The girls froze, eyes wide, as if they'd just witnessed a crime scene. And there was Mark, laughing uncontrollably, completely unbothered. They gave him a death stare that could've melted brick.

I laid there, partly stunned, partly humiliated, but mostly trying not to laugh, too. Because as reckless as it all was, this was Mark. He didn't pity me. He didn't walk on eggshells. He treated me like one of the guys—maybe too much like one of the guys, but I wouldn't have traded it. I was learning that sometimes friends pull you into chaos, but I wondered who would run in when life swept me under?

Life with my roommates swung from moments of pure comedy to stretches of ordinary routine, late nights of Sega Genesis, trash talk, and laughter echoing through our apartment. It felt like our little world was sealed off from the bigger problems beyond campus, a bubble of youth and friendship where nothing serious could really reach us.

But that illusion shattered in an instant. One night, in the middle of our usual gaming marathon, a stranger pounded on the door. When we opened it, a man stood there with a shotgun, yelling, "You guys gotta get out of here!" Then he bolted into the night. Mark and I stared at each other in disbelief. What was going on? We stepped outside, and the smell of smoke hit us before we saw the orange glow. Buildings were burning just blocks away. My sheltered world came to a halt. The Los Angeles Riots had begun.

Following the shooting of Latasha Harlins in 1991, the Rodney King beating highlighted the buildup of racial tensions and police brutality in Los Angeles. When an all-white jury acquitted the four officers on April 29, 1992, the city erupted. Looting, burning buildings, assaults, and violent confrontations with law enforcement spread rapidly. From campus, we could see flames lighting up the night sky and smell the smoke drifting across the city. Classes were canceled, and we were told to isolate indoors.

But my roommates decided not to wait. We threw a few things together and headed for Mark's parents' house in Orange. As we sat in the car, inching through streets that no longer felt safe, silence filled the space between us. Around every corner, uncertainty waited. Groups spilled into the roads. Some shouting. Some smashing windows. My chest tightened as an old, familiar feeling surfaced. It wasn't only fear of what was happening around us. It was the same paralyzing terror I'd felt as a child in Saigon, when chaos erupted without warning.

In that instant, the smell of smoke in Los Angeles collided with the memory of smoke in Vietnam. The fear felt eerily the same: *Will I survive this?*

There were police in riot gear everywhere, pushing forward on the streets as they shoved rioters back. Looters were smashing store windows as hundreds ran in and out with clothes, shoes, and whatever they could grab. As I looked out the back window of the car, I watched our favorite Block Buster Video store burn to the ground, but at least the riots were behind us.

We finally made it to the Schmidts' house where they greeted us and made us some food to calm our nerves. We were alive. And it was here that I would meet my second parents, people who would open their home and hearts to me in ways that left a lasting imprint. In the middle of chaos, Mark Sr. and Jan became a reminder that family isn't just who you're born to; it's also who takes you in when you need it most. They would meet my needs many times throughout my adult life.

A few days later, school resumed with the presence of the National Guard near campus. When Mark and I returned to our apartment, everything was unscathed, almost as if nothing had happened. But I wasn't the same. My uneasiness lingered, even as everyone else seemed to move on. Still, like so many times before, I found myself pressing forward—choosing resilience over fear.

Looking back, I realize the riots weren't only about that night in Los Angeles. They were about a system broken for generations. The shooting of Latasha Harlins. The acquittal of the officers in the Rodney King beating. Both exposed wounds in our community that had been ignored for too long. Sitting in that car, I felt fear. But I also began to understand something I hadn't before. Fear was the daily reality for so many who lived in neighborhoods scarred by violence and poverty. For them, this wasn't just one chaotic night. It was life.

That realization planted something in me. Just as I had been lifted from the chaos of Saigon into safety, I began to see that leadership must be about lifting others from the chaos in their lives. Whether that chaos comes from poverty, discrimination, or trauma, the role of a leader is not to look away, but to step in and create pathways to safety and hope. The riots reminded me that when people feel unseen for too long, the pain eventually erupts. Years later, as a superintendent, that lesson stayed with me. Students must feel seen, valued, and included, or their potential will be crushed under the weight of being ignored.

When classes eventually resumed, I found myself clinging to the routine as a way of regaining balance. Returning to lectures and business case studies felt almost trivial compared to what had just shaken the city, but it was also grounding. Normalcy became a kind of refuge, reminding me that even in the midst of upheaval, life kept moving forward.

Amid the chaos and comedy of life with Mark, another part of me was beginning to stir, something quieter, deeper. While my social world was full of energy and unpredictability, I started craving direction. Purpose. I still dreamed of becoming a businessman, but I began to wonder: What kind of man did I want to be? I'd find my answer in a classroom, thanks to a professor who would shift the trajectory of my thinking entirely. That's when I met Mac Davis.

When I came to USC, I was laser-focused on becoming a successful business owner. I wanted to build something. Grow something. Make a name for myself. Mac wasn't just a professor. He was a real-world entrepreneur who ran a successful retail business in Colorado. Every week, he flew to USC to teach. On weekends, he flew home to manage his company. He didn't teach from theory. He taught from experience.

What struck me most wasn't how much he knew about business. It was how much he understood about people. He told us the most successful business leaders weren't necessarily the smartest in the room. Instead, they were people who raised others. People who saw potential and built teams around strengths. People who made others feel valued. That idea cracked something open in me.

For the first time, I saw leadership not as a title but as a responsibility, an invitation to bring others along. I still learned how to write a business plan, measure profit, and take risks, but the real lesson Mac gave me was this: *If you want to go far, take people with you.*

Photo of Mac Davis, who taught the entrepreneur program.
From Stefan Bean's personal photo library.

While Mac taught me how to lead others with vision and heart, another professor helped me develop the voice to do it. Leadership, I was learning, wasn't just about strategy. It was about connection. And connection starts with communication. Professor Laree Kylee led the business communication course for my minor. Her classroom became a training ground for one of my most important skills: connecting with people. She pushed us far beyond reading from notecards or rehearsing memorized speeches. At first, it felt awkward, even silly. But soon, I realized she was teaching us to do something far more important: to be seen and heard—to hold space in a room without overpowering it. Those lessons would follow me into interviews, boardrooms, classrooms, and stages for the rest of my life. Like a coach for the real world, she challenged us to think on our feet, speak with presence, and persuade with authenticity, even if we were just selling someone a pen.

Professor Davis and Professor Kylee's lessons lit a fire within me, and maybe gave me a little too much confidence. Inspired by their classes and what I'd learned in marketing, I decided to try my hand at entrepreneurship. With one click, I ordered five hundred "elegant" pens, convinced I could sell them with the same flair I'd practiced in class.

When the box arrived, my heart sank. They were cheap, flimsy, and embarrassing. I'd been scammed. Not one sold. Not even to my friends. What started as a burst of enthusiasm turned into my first real taste of failure in business. Up to that point, I had never really failed, at least not like this. I was used to effort leading to results, passion leading to progress. But this time, enthusiasm had overpowered wisdom, and I had skipped the most important steps: research, planning, listening. I'd learned in class about market testing, customer interviews, and understanding your audience, but I didn't apply any of it.

That failure stung. Not because of lost money, but because it exposed a blind spot. It taught me that leadership is not just confidence. It's about curiosity. It's about slowing down enough to ask the right questions and listening to the customer before trying to sell the solution. I took the loss, bruised ego and all, and moved forward. Smarter. More grounded. A little more humble.

Around that time, Mark and I were both taking a business communication course. He was actually a great speaker: clear, funny, articulate. But it made him incredibly nervous. Every time he got up to present, he'd sweat through his shirt and shake his head afterward like he'd just survived something traumatic. He was always amazed at how easily I could speak off the cuff, how comfortable I seemed in front of a crowd. Maybe it was that first deodorant commercial, flakes and all, that convinced me I could wing it in front of anyone.

His reaction made me more aware of my own comfort in that space, and I started wondering how I could push that strength even further. Not just in class, but in something bigger. That's when I was invited to take on a new project that would test everything I was learning: *Song Fest*. It wasn't just a student event; it was a full production. And I was asked to lead it.

Our fraternity teamed up with a sorority to produce *Song Fest*, a high-energy student musical competition at the legendary Shrine Auditorium. I was asked to take the lead as producer and director. At first, the title sounded exciting. Then I realized it meant managing everything: writing the script, directing a cast of over fifty students, coordinating choreography, running full-scale rehearsals. It was massive. But it was the kind of challenge I was starting to crave.

Thankfully, I had an extraordinary team. Two of my classmates, Chris and Tim, composed original music for the entire show. They weren't just talented—they were brilliant. Years later, they'd go on to compose major soundtracks for Marvel films, hit TV shows, and even the wildly popular series *The Boys*. Even then, I knew they were destined for something great. Mark's mom, an accomplished singer, helped arrange and coach our choir, bringing vocal discipline and polish to the performance.

I knew I had bitten off more than I could chew, but instead of trying to carry it alone, I leaned into something Mac Davis had taught me: delegate, empower, and trust. I focused on organizing, encouraging, and drawing the best out of people. Song Fest didn't just teach me how to manage a production; it showed me how to lead one.

Rehearsals ran like clockwork. The cast was sharp, the timing crisp, and the chemistry electric. I felt proud because we had built something beautiful together. The night of the event arrived, and the atmosphere was electric. The Shrine Auditorium was packed. Women arrived in elegant dresses and heels, men in suits and ties, the energy buzzing with anticipation. As the lights dimmed and the curtains pulled back, I took a deep breath. This was it.

But then everything started to unravel. The music cued late. The timing was off. Heads turned in confusion as entrances missed their marks and choreography lagged behind the beat. The sound system betrayed us, throwing off cues we had rehearsed to perfection. What we had practiced flawlessly now felt like chaos unfolding in slow motion. I sat there, helpless, watching our cast struggle to keep up with a rhythm they couldn't hear.

After the curtain closed, people came up to congratulate us with kind words and a few compliments on how we held it together despite the sound issues. But I wasn't feeling gracious. I was furious. I had poured everything into this production. We all had. And despite the praise, we didn't receive a single award. Not even formal recognition.

I let my frustration show. In front of the very people who had given their time, talent, and heart to this project, I lost my cool. I didn't yell or blame, but the disappointment poured out of me in ways I couldn't reel back. I had never experienced failure on this scale, at least not one so public and so raw. It was my first real taste of what it felt like to lead something that didn't go as planned. The first time, I didn't win. And I didn't handle it well.

After the adrenaline wore off, embarrassment set in. I replayed my reaction in my head and felt a wave of regret, not because I had cared too much, but because I had forgotten to care about the right things. I had let the outcome overshadow the process. The truth was, we had pulled off something extraordinary. We created a show from scratch, rallied dozens of people, and overcame obstacles we never saw coming.

I took responsibility. I went back and apologized to the cast, our sorority partners, and everyone who had worked tirelessly to bring the show to life. They deserved more than my frustration. They deserved my gratitude. That moment taught me something I carry with me still: leadership isn't about controlling the outcome. It's about honoring the process, lifting up the people who make it happen, and learning how to lose with grace.

After the intensity of *Song Fest*, I was grateful to return to something familiar. My routine at the Lyon Center—working shifts, seeing friends, studying—felt steadying. I needed that rhythm. It grounded me. And through it all, Janet was still there.

Our friendship had deepened into something rich and easy. We could talk for hours. About my chaotic upbringing. About her life on the farm. About our shared struggles with classes we barely tolerated. We laughed about professors. Swapped stories about campus parties neither of us actually attended. Joked about being the only two sober people in every room.

But it wasn't just laughter and small talk. We talked about the future, our dreams and our fears, and what we wanted from life. I didn't realize it then, but those conversations were planting something quietly and steadily beneath the surface: a connection built not on drama or sparks, but on trust.

The more time I spent with Janet, the harder it became to ignore what was happening inside me. At first, it was just easy conversation, shared jokes, and mutual respect. But somewhere along the way, it shifted. I started looking for her without realizing it, scanning the gym for her face, feeling disappointed when our shifts didn't overlap, and feeling lighter when they did.

It hit me one night as we stood outside after a long shift. She laughed at something I said. Tilted her head just slightly. Her eyes squinted, and her whole face, soft and real. And I felt it. Not butterflies. Not infatuation. Something deeper. Familiar. Safe. It wasn't a rush like it had been with Shannon. It was a quiet knowing.

I realized I didn't just enjoy being around Janet. I needed it. That terrified me. Because this time, it wasn't about proving anything or chasing a fantasy. It was about risking something real.

Janet and I kept growing closer. With each shift we worked, the connection felt more undeniable. Quiet. Steady. Wrapped in the kind of warmth that doesn't demand attention but commands it. I caught myself looking forward to her in ways I hadn't expected. The sound of her laugh. The way she looked at me when I spoke. It all began to matter.

So one day, I decided to stop wondering and start risking. She showed up to work wearing jeans and a T-shirt—simple, effortless, and somehow beautiful. Her dark hair framed her soft brown eyes, which, as always, radiated kindness. We were talking about a party coming up when I paused, took a breath, and asked, "Janet…would you go out with me?

LIFTED Value: **Develop Others** True leadership is measured not by what happens during your tenure, but by the leaders you raise for the future. Mentorship, coaching, and intentional investment in people ensure that the mission will continue long after you are gone.

Lifted Insight:

"*I took responsibility. I went back and apologized to the cast, our sorority partners, and everyone who had worked tirelessly to bring the show to life. They deserved more than my frustration. They deserved my gratitude. That moment taught me something I carry with me still: leadership isn't about controlling the outcome. It's about honoring the process, lifting up the people who make it happen, and learning how to lose with grace.*"

Leadership Reflection: When have you turned a leadership mistake into an opportunity to develop others (or yourself)?

CHAPTER 7

~

Love Deferred, Faith Preserved

She said, "No."

She said it so plainly, so quietly, that for a split second I wondered if I'd misheard her. All I could hear was the buzz from the air conditioner, drowned out by women laughing and talking as they sprinted around the perimeter of the gym. When Janet said no, the room felt like it was caving in on me, and the smell of sweat from the football players lifting weights made me nauseous.

What? I couldn't believe it. I thought we had a strong connection. We'd spent hours at the Lyon Center working together, talking, sharing details about our lives. I was sure we were on the same page. But apparently, I was the only one who saw it that way. Inside, my head was shaking, saying, "No, this can't be right." Outwardly, I tried to keep my face neutral, but it felt like the floor had just dropped out from under me.

I was more surprised than anything, and I worried it was written all over my face for everyone to see. It reminded me of asking my mom for a second piece of cake as a kid and with no hesitation, no drama, she simply said no. Janet didn't flinch or try to soften her response.

She simply said no. I left the gym that day feeling deflated, but I later realized even rejection has something to teach us if we're willing to listen. Her "no" forced me to confront my own assumptions, to hear a reality I didn't want to hear, and to begin learning how to grow through disappointment.

Meanwhile, I was working overtime to look calm, but my mind was scrambling, replaying every laugh we'd shared, every late-night conversation, wondering how I could have read it all so wrong. Janet didn't seem the least bit embarrassed that I'd put her in this position, or that it might change our friendship. If anything, it felt like she'd rehearsed this moment. Her answer was ready, her tone steady. She was operating in a place of certainty, while I was sitting there feeling blindsided, hurt, and suddenly unsure of where I stood with her at all. Even then, some quiet part of me still trusted she'd show up when it mattered most.

I made awkward small talk with her until our shift at the Lyon Center finally ended, both of us pretending nothing had just happened. The second I rolled out of the gym, the impact of it hit me. I felt like a deflated tire that had once been solid and steady. Everything that had been holding me up—the hope, the excitement—was gone, and I was just trying to make it back to my apartment without showing how flat I really felt.

Until that day, we were almost inseparable. We worked the same shifts, grabbed dinner afterward, showed up at the same parties with our mutual friends, and even had those lazy hangouts where nothing much happened but it still felt like time well spent. It was easy, comfortable, and I thought it was leading somewhere. After she said no, it was like a switch flipped. I couldn't imagine things going back to how they'd been.

Once the shock wore off, it left behind a dull ache that I couldn't shake. I stopped asking her to grab dinner or go to parties, and decided I'd only see her when our shifts overlapped. Part of me wanted to punish her for not feeling the same way, but mostly, I was just protecting myself. If I kept my distance, maybe I could keep the rejection from replaying in my head every time we talked.

This felt like the same story playing out all over again, another chapter in a pattern I couldn't seem to break. It made me wonder if I was destined to always be the friend, never the one chosen. So I did what I knew how to do: pull back, shut the door, and lock my heart away before it could take another hit. Not only did I quit pursuing her, but I was also actually *not very nice* to her when we worked together. I told myself in a cocky way that since she had put me in the friend zone, that's exactly where I'd keep it.

The party I'd invited her to wasn't just some random get-together. It was the Trojan Knights formal, one of the biggest events my senior year. The timing couldn't have been worse. She had ruined my chances of bringing a date. The Knights weren't just another club; they were a tight brotherhood, like my fraternity, built on tradition and pride. Getting invited to join was an honor, and the formal was the kind of night you didn't want to show up to alone. But now, that's exactly what I was watching.

The Knights were USC's historic brotherhood of tradition and pride, and the formal was the biggest event of the year. Every guy I talked to already had a date lined up, and the last thing I wanted was to roll in solo. I ran through every possible name in my head, but nobody felt right to take to this event. The truth was, even after pulling back and trying to keep my distance, Janet was still there in the back of my mind. I didn't want her to be, but she was. And with no one else I really wanted to bring, I ended up going alone.

The boat glowed at sunset, twinkle lights wrapping the railings. Everyone looked like they belonged, except me, alone. The guys were sharp in tuxedos, the women looked like they'd stepped out of a magazine in their long gowns. I tried to take it all in, but in the back of my mind I kept noticing what was missing. I didn't have anyone on my arm. My brothers pulled me into conversations and laughs, but I couldn't shake the feeling that I stuck out. Eventually, after making the rounds, I drifted to the corner of the boat and stayed there, watching the water, trying not to look as alone as I felt.

After that night on the boat, I slipped right back into my new routine with Janet—polite but distant. At work, she'd try small talk, and I'd act like I didn't hear her or keep my eyes on whatever I was doing. When our shift ended, I'd say a quick goodbye and roll out, no hanging around on the bleachers like we used to. I told myself it was about moving on, but really, I was just guarding what was left of my pride.

I realized I was lonely, even with friends around me. Some women showed interest. I went on a few dates. But none of it felt the same. I missed what Janet and I had. Not just flirting. Not just hoping for something more. I missed how we could talk for hours about anything. Losing that was bigger than losing a chance at dating her. It was like a part of my daily life had gone quiet.

Life felt different without Janet. The more I tried to push her out of my mind, the more I caught myself wanting her around. I realized I didn't need her to be my girlfriend. I just wanted her back in my daily life. So I asked her to grab dinner once in a while. We went to a few parties together, like before. It wasn't the same, but it was better than pretending we had nothing. Eventually, I accepted that maybe this was all we'd ever be. Friends. And I tried to make peace with that.

> I realized I didn't need her to be my girlfriend. I just wanted her back in my daily life.

One afternoon, we slipped back into our old rhythm. She walked the track. I wheeled beside her. The sun was out, a light breeze cutting the warmth just enough to make it comfortable. Out of nowhere she asked, "Stefan, what happened to our friendship?" Like she'd been holding on to that question for a long time. I told her the truth. "I was hurt. I thought we were on the same page and ready to take the next step."

88

Maybe it was the way she looked at me, or the urgency in her voice, but something in me lit back up. Before I could overthink it, I asked, "Are you ready now?" For a split second, I felt like the confident, persistent version of myself who had pushed past the hurt. We stopped at the bleachers. She sat down, brushing her dark hair from her face, her expression turning serious. "Stefan," she said, "I'm a junior. You're graduating. I have one more year here. You'll be moving on with your life, and I'll still be here keeping my promise to my parents that I will graduate."

My heart sank. Was she giving me hope just to take it away again, or was I the one reading it wrong? I glanced toward a tree beside the bleachers, crowded with blackbirds shifting restlessly on the branches. "We can make this work," I told her, my voice tight but steady. The birds kept moving, wings rustling, mimicking my impatience for an answer. "I can't. I need to focus on my studies," she said, and walked off.

Later that night, I sat in my room, still and quiet, like a display no one stopped to look at. No music, no TV, just me and the enormity of the conversation. Deep down, I knew how hard she'd worked to get to USC. She didn't have financial help from her parents, and every day here was something she was fighting for. The truth was, she told me from the start she was here for two things: her degree and to grow closer to God. I didn't want to hear it. But sitting there, I had to admit she was probably right. I was a distraction from what mattered most to her.

Over the next few days, I forced myself out of the slump. Not because I felt better. But because life kept moving, whether I wanted it to or not. I kept telling myself Janet and I could still be good friends, like repeating it enough times might make it feel true. Accepting that was the only way I could figure out how to move forward.

My senior year was winding down, graduation getting closer with every week. I didn't want to finish it sitting around thinking about what I couldn't change with Janet. So I shifted my focus to what I could control: making the most of my last months on campus. That meant more time with my roommates, more parties, and saying yes to just about anything that might keep my mind busy. Our apartment was right in the middle of the party scene, and there were plenty of them. Matt, Jeff, Jason "Bear," Mark, and my other roommates were master planners—Mark and Jeff got the word out, Matt scored the beer, and Bear made room by shoving furniture around, pausing now and then to scratch his back on the corner of the wall.

When we weren't throwing parties, we crammed into the living room for Sega Genesis marathons. We fought over Sega games with the same intensity as any frat rivalry. So I threw myself into parties, video games, and other women. Anything to keep my mind off Janet.

That's when I met Julie. She was a lot of fun and wasn't shy about flirting. She looked great in a tiny black dress with her brown curly hair. She was full of energy and positivity—just what I needed to keep my mind elsewhere. Julie would get out on the dance floor and dance with me, wheelchair and all, making sure I had a great time. She'd later date Mark for a short time, but for that night, she made me forget about Janet.

As graduation got closer, I kept myself busy, wrapping up my classes, polishing my business plan, and spending time with the guys. There were social events here and there, but school was my priority. Every so often, Janet would show up at something I was at, and it always threw me off. I'd start out confident, but by the time I opened my mouth to say something, I'd be stumbling over my words like a freshman again.

With finals behind us and graduation just days away, my roommates and I decided to host one last get-together before we all went our separate ways. It wasn't about throwing the wildest party of the year, but more of a send-off for friends we might not see again. I called my brother Martin, who was back finishing his last year of medical school, and told him to stop by. He didn't come expecting much—just a few people, some music, and a chance to catch up.

That night, we set out a couple of kegs, some snacks in bowls, and a few flashing lights in the courtyard to make it feel festive. What began as a small send-off quickly swelled into a courtyard packed shoulder to shoulder. Somewhere in the middle of it all, I heard two people yelling from across the courtyard. I glanced at Martin, ready for him to roll his eyes or tell me the party had gotten out of hand. Instead, he just grinned and said, "Wow, Stefan, I didn't know you had it in you." He was clearly having a blast, and honestly, so was everyone else. I started looking around and realized there were many faces I didn't even recognize.

Photo of Stefan, Martin, and friends at graduation party.
Photo from Stefan's personal photo album.

The last thing I expected was to see USC football team members walk through the door. Word must have spread faster than I could keep track. My chest tightened. Part of me was pumped to see it turn into something this big, and part of me was wondering how in the world I was going to keep it from going sideways. I didn't have to wonder for long. Red and blue lights flashed across the walls as the police pulled up, their voice booming over the loudspeaker: "Attention! This is an unlawful gathering. You are ordered to disperse immediately." The crowd groaned like a game had just been called early.

In the days that followed, people wouldn't stop talking about it. Friends, classmates, even people I barely knew swore it was the biggest party USC had seen in decades. Some called it legendary. Others said they'd never seen that many people in one place without it being a football game. We hadn't planned for it to turn into campus history, but somehow it did and our names were attached to it. Then, just like that, the buzz died down, and all that was left was graduation day staring me in the face.

Graduation day couldn't have been different. Just a week earlier, the courtyard had been packed with music, laughter, and the chaos of the biggest party in years. Now I was sitting in my cap and gown, surrounded by rows of classmates in neat lines, the air filled with the sound of speeches instead of bass. I felt a swirl of emotions. Proud I'd made it. Relieved to be done. Sad to leave friends behind. Nervous about entering the real world.

The stage was draped in USC's cardinal and gold, the School of Business Administration banner hanging proudly behind rows of faculty in their academic robes. As I waited for my name, I couldn't help but think about the road that led me here, from an orphanage in Vietnam, to being lifted by friends up staircases in school, to Mr. Geisinger insisting I give oral presentations when writing felt impossible, building my confidence one assignment at a time. I thought about every setback, every "no," every moment I thought I'd reached my limit had somehow carried me to this stage. When it was my turn, I rolled forward in my pink wheelchair, hand outstretched for the handshake. I did it. Tears welled up as I thought about everyone who had lifted me, literally and figuratively, to this moment.

Photo of Stefan's graduation at USC.
Photo from Stefan's personal photo album. 1993.

When the ceremony ended, we moved our tassels to the other side, and hats flew into the air like a burst of freedom. I looked around at my classmates. Some were laughing. Some were crying. We all knew this chapter was over. For me, it wasn't just the end of college; it was the payoff of years of being lifted by others, from the orphanage to this very stage. I felt proud, grateful, and a little stunned that I had actually made it. But as the crowd broke into hugs and photo ops, I couldn't help noticing who wasn't there. Janet hadn't come.

After the ceremony, reality hit fast. I sent out résumés, went to interviews, and heard, "We'll be in touch" more times than I could count. Most never called back. One interviewer finally gave me a reason. They didn't think I could handle the travel the job required. They didn't say it outright, but I knew what they meant: the wheelchair. It stung, not because I thought I was entitled to the job, but because they didn't even give me the chance to prove them wrong. So when a recruiter called offering me a position as an assistant buyer for Robinsons May, I was

Photo of Stefan and Laurie at USC graduation.
Photo from the personal photo album of Stefan Bean. 1993.

ready to grab it. It felt like a door opening after a hallway of slammed ones.

The job was close enough to my apartment that moving didn't make sense, so I decided to stay put for at least another year. It was practical. A shorter commute. A familiar neighborhood. But I can't pretend it didn't cross my mind that Janet still had her senior year ahead of her. Even if we weren't anything more than friends, being nearby felt like keeping a door cracked open.

After graduation, actually seeing Janet turned out to be harder than I expected. She was busy on the medical campus, buried in classes and labs, while I was off campus working full-time. We'd catch each other on the phone now and then or run into each other at a party, but it wasn't enough. Every time we talked, I wanted her to know I was still in her corner—that if she ever needed me, I'd show up.

Then one day, Janet called me in tears. One of her roommates had taken her own life. She was shaken, her voice breaking as she told me they'd been close, always talking, and she kept saying she should have noticed something, and should have done more. I told her it wasn't her fault, that sometimes people hide their pain so well no one sees it, but my words didn't seem to reach her. At that moment, I didn't care about saying the perfect thing; I just wanted her to feel that she wasn't alone.

After that call, I tried to check in on her as often as I could. Sometimes she'd pick up, but her voice sounded flat, drained of the energy I was used to. Other times she wouldn't answer at all. She barely left her dorm except for class, and I could hear in her tone that she was shutting the world out. Each time I hung up, I felt a little more uneasy, like something bigger was going on that she wasn't telling me.

Janet's graduation came not long after her roommate's suicide, and she invited me to attend. Part of me still felt the sting that she hadn't come to mine, but I knew how much this day meant to her. After everything she'd just been through, there was no way I wasn't going to be there. She walked across the stage looking pale and worn down, but when she spotted me afterward, she smiled. I handed her a small gift and told her how proud I was. Things between us weren't what I once hoped, but showing up for her felt like the right thing to do.

After graduation, Janet decided to stay at USC to begin her master's program in Occupational Therapy. By the time her first year was underway, the pressure of everything she'd been through was catching up to her. She was carrying the demands of grad school, the loss of her roommate, and the isolation that came from pulling back from almost everyone.

I tried calling her a couple of times, but there was no answer and no call back. At first, I told myself she was just busy with grad school, but the silence started to feel heavy. Then I heard from her sister, Lucy, that Janet had been hospitalized. My heart dropped.

I raced to the hospital, not knowing what I'd find. When I walked in, I learned she'd been battling walking pneumonia for weeks, and the antibiotics she'd been given weren't strong enough to knock it out. After her roommate's death, she had shut herself away in her dorm with no one checking in on her. I kept thinking, *Did she even realize how sick she was? Or had she been too deep in grief to notice?*

When I finally entered her hospital room, the sight of her stopped me cold. Janet looked so small in that bed. She was pale. She was exhausted. She was nothing like the strong, determined woman I was used to seeing. Her eyes were glassy, drifting past me like she wasn't fully present. I rolled my chair closer, searching for something to say that would pull her back, but nothing came. I just sat there, willing her to feel that she wasn't alone.

At one point, she turned to me and said, almost matter-of-factly, "Stefan, I don't think I can marry you because when I'm older and sick, you won't be able to care for me." The words hit me like a punch. My first instinct was to tell her she was wrong and that I would do anything for her. But as the silence stretched between us, a different thought crept in, one I didn't want to admit even to myself: *maybe she was right.* The reality of my disability flashed in my mind. The physical things I couldn't do, the ways I might fall short if she ever needed the kind of care that required lifting or constant physical help. I hated that doubt. I wanted to believe love and commitment would be enough, but at that moment, I wasn't sure.

I left that day knowing she was facing more than just a physical illness. Something in her spirit had been worn down, and part of me wondered if there would be a time in the future when she'd need someone to be there for her in an even greater way.

I spoke with her sister, Lucy, in the hallway. "What happened?" I asked. She said she wasn't completely sure. Janet had always been the strong one in the family. Lucy thought the pressure of Janet's first year of grad school, the walking pneumonia, lack of sleep, and the trauma of her roommate's suicide had all piled on her at once. Later, I learned there was even more to it: another roommate had treated Janet terribly and had gone as far as to blame her for the suicide. Knowing that made it clear just how much she'd been carrying.

I visited her as often as I could while she was in the hospital. Some days she would talk a little, other days she would just stare past me, lost in her own thoughts. I never knew which version of her I'd get, but it didn't matter because I just wanted her to know I was there. I'd sit by her bed, sometimes in silence, sometimes trying to draw her out with stories or small jokes, hoping for even the slightest smile. Watching someone you care about so deeply in that state is a helpless feeling, like you'd give anything to trade places with them just so they could have a break from the pain. Even in her weakness, when she barely spoke, she let me sit beside her. Sometimes presence is its own kind of yes.

By the end of her first year in grad school, she was still pale and weak, trying to recover from everything that had happened. One afternoon, we sat together on a bench under a giant tree, the sunlight breaking through the branches and falling across her face. She looked at me and said, "Stefan, I'm going home for a while. I need to heal."

As much as I hated the thought of her being all the way in Lemoore while I stayed in Los Angeles, I didn't hesitate to say, "I understand. I just want you to get well." So she left.

With Janet back in Lemoore and most of my friends graduated, the world around me seemed to shrink. Mark and I found our own place off campus, but it felt nothing like the old apartment. The constant stream of people, the parties, the late-night video game marathons—all of it was gone. I'd go to work, come home, and the silence would settle in. Mark and I got along fine, but the energy was different. I missed the easy chaos of my old crew, and even more, I knew Janet was a long drive away.

We still talked on the phone from time to time, and those calls became the highlight of my week. She told me that being home gave her a chance to rest and sleep as much as she needed. Slowly, she said, she was starting to feel more like herself. Hearing that was a relief, not just because I wanted her to be OK, but because I could hear some life back in her voice. It made the distance feel a little smaller, even if she was still hours away.

As she grew stronger, our conversations turned into plans. We both admitted we missed seeing each other in person, and neither of us hesitated at the idea of driving the hours it would take to meet halfway. Bakersfield was the natural choice. My best friend from high school, Eric Falk, lived there with his wife, Sandy now, and they were happy to have us stay. Just knowing we were both willing to make the trip gave me hope. Knowing she wanted to see me as much as I wanted to see her made me believe our story wasn't finished.

When Janet walked through Eric and Sandy's door, I walked toward her in my crutches and gave her a long hug, holding on just a second longer than usual. She looked healthy again, with color back in her cheeks, eyes clear, and her voice carrying the familiar energy I'd missed. Eric and Sandy welcomed her like family, and the four of us fell into easy conversation over Sandy's home-cooked meals. Later, Eric and I swapped old high school stories while Janet laughed along, sometimes jumping in with her own jokes. It felt good, like we'd picked up right where we left off, only this time with the distance behind us.

After that first trip, meeting in Bakersfield became our thing. Every few months, one of us would call and say, "It's about that time," and we'd both clear our schedules. It didn't matter how busy life got. She made the drive from Lemoore, I made it from Los Angeles, and we'd land in the middle like it was our own little checkpoint. Those weekends gave me something to look forward to, a break from routine, and a reminder that no matter the distance, we were still choosing to show up for each other.

One night, after everyone had gone to bed, Janet and I stayed up talking on our air mattresses in the living room. The house was quiet, the kind of stillness where every whisper feels amplified. At some point, she rolled onto her side and began rubbing my back. My heart pumped loudly. Maybe it was nothing, just a friendly gesture, but it felt different. When she stopped, I shifted closer and began massaging her shoulders in return. For a few minutes, neither of us said anything, just the sound of our breathing and the faint hum of the refrigerator in the background. My mind was spinning. *Is this just comfort between friends, or is something changing?* Finally, I broke the silence.

"Janet, is something more happening here?"

She looked at me, her eyes steady on mine…

LIFTED Value: **Listen and Learn** True leadership does not begin with a plan or a directive, it begins with paying attention to the voice of others.

Lifted Insight:

"Janet didn't flinch or try to soften her response. She simply said no. I left the gym that day feeling deflated, but I later realized even rejection has something to teach us if we're willing to listen. Her "no" forced me to confront my own assumptions, to hear a reality I didn't want to hear, and to begin learning how to grow through disappointment."

Leadership Reflection: What lessons have you learned from difficult stories you've listened to, and how have they influenced your leadership approach?

CHAPTER 8

Miracles in Motion

Janet whispered, "No Stefan. You're such a dear friend to me, someone I know I can always count on. I treasure our talks and the time we spend together and it means more than you know. We're just friends."

Wow! I had never been so confused in my life.

It hit me instantly. I had reached my limit. I was done trying to pursue her. Janet and I were never going to be more than just good friends. This quiet realization sank in as I rolled over and went to sleep that night, just wanting to forget any of this happened.

The drive home was a blur of highway lines and simmering frustration. Janet had side-lined me once again, and the familiar ache of rejection gnawed at me. *How many times did this have to happen for me to finally get it?* Each mile marker seemed to mock my stubborn pursuit, stripping away any lingering hope I'd clung to.

The "just friends" blow landed hard, and in its wake, I felt an unfamiliar restlessness. My role as an assistant buyer, once a steady anchor, now felt suffocating. It wasn't just the rejection from Janet; it was a deeper realization that my life needed a seismic shift. Within weeks of that crushing conversation, I made the impulsive, terrifying decision: I was done with the corporate grind. My new path? Starting my own software company. It felt like burning all my bridges, leaving behind everything familiar in a single, defiant act.

Larry Chen, a brilliant software developer, along with partners and I, poured ourselves into creating software that would allow multiple users to collaborate on the same document or platform simultaneously. We were convinced it was revolutionary. But pitch after pitch, we hit the same wall. "Great concept," they'd say, "but the bandwidth isn't there to support it." Each rejection felt like another punch, echoing the one Janet had delivered. We were ahead of our time, and it was crushing.

Now what am I going to do? I had no clue. No girl; and the direction of my business venture had changed drastically. I was struggling. The only thing I could do was go on a road trip by myself. I needed time away from the disappointment of Janet, and the turmoil of my failed business venture to clear my head. I drove north up the Western coastline, the Pacific stretching beside me, Jim Croce on the stereo. With the sun on my face and ocean air rushing in, my thoughts finally began to untangle.

Am I making a big mistake starting my own business? Janet doesn't think of me as I think of her. I think she loves me as a friend, but I just love her. God, I'm praying for wisdom and your guidance as I take my next steps. You've always been there for me and have shown me the way. I trust you.

I stopped at a beautiful restaurant overlooking the ocean as thoughts continued racing in my head. While I ate clam chowder and a fancy steak dinner, I watched the sun set. I finally had clarity and a sense of acceptance. I knew what I had to do.

My roommate Mark told me his parents were renting a room in the house we stayed in during the L.A. Riots. It was an upstairs room that was laid out like a mini apartment. After meeting them before, I didn't question deciding to move in and save money for a while, so I could heal my wounded heart and contemplate my next project.

Mark Sr. was quiet, kind, and steady, the sort of man whose presence brought calm to any room. Jan was his opposite. She was outgoing, full of energy, and quick to draw people in with her warmth. Together, their differences didn't divide them; they harmonized. She loved classical music, he loved jazz, yet somehow their lives played like one song. They hosted gatherings where her laughter lit the room and his gentle smile anchored it, creating a rhythm uniquely their own. Watching them across the dinner table, sharing a glance, a laugh, or a simple touch, I saw the kind of enduring partnership I longed for, a marriage woven from contrast yet filled with grace, balance, and unwavering love.

Jan, an albino with white hair, was the musician and singer who had helped me during *Song Fest*. The Schmidts were a very loving couple who welcomed me with open arms, right when I needed the comfort of a home.

I went to settle in my room. The house was grand, quiet, and far more affluent than anything I had known as a child. Soft jazz played in the background. It wasn't the house that reminded me of home, it was Jan. She was kind and funny and never let me get away with anything. Her presence carried the same mix of love and strength my mom had once given me, and that was enough to make me feel at home.

Mark Sr. was concerned that my room was at the top of the stairs, and he wondered how I would manage going up and down. I reassured him without hesitation, pulling myself up as I had done so many times before. His shocked look was priceless. Later, he asked how I did it with such ease, and I told him simply, "I've had a lot of practice." My room was simple, clean, and just right for me. After months of emotional turbulence and professional uncertainty, I felt a surprising sense of peace settling in. For the first time in a long while, I was genuinely happy to call a place home.

That sense of stability gave me space to reopen relationships around me. One afternoon the phone rang, and it was my old roommate, Matt Dittrich. His voice carried the excitement of someone whose life was changing. "Hey Stefan, guess what? I'm getting married!" I had introduced Matt to Kim, a girl from church, and they had clicked right away.

Hearing the joy in his voice made me smile. "Wow, Matt, that's incredible," I said.

Then he added words that humbled me: "Stefan, will you be my best man?"

I didn't hesitate. Of course I answered yes. Matt and I had been roommates for years, and our friendship had been built on countless late-night conversations, endless poker games, and a respect for each other's strengths. He was a brilliant, nerdy engineer with a sharp mind and a loyal heart. Over time, we had become more than just roommates; we had become brothers.

A thought crossed my mind. *Jason, Mark, and Eric were all married, and now it was Matt.* Having been a groomsman in their weddings was an honor for me, yet with each one, it made me wonder if I would ever be a groom. With every best man's toast, it seemed my childhood dream of getting married and having a family was someone's after thought, lingering in the background. *Hopeless.*

Soon I found out that Janet would be coming down for the wedding. She and Matt had graduated in the same class together and were good friends, so naturally he would invite her. I tried to decipher the sense of excitement and dread that came over me all at once. I was just beginning to clear my head about my relationship with Janet. Even though we talked all the time, it was easier to be "just friends" when she was a long distance away. It had been awhile since our last face-to-face. Right now, I didn't trust myself to be around her without longing for more.

The church was beautiful with light streaming through the stained-glass windows when Matt's wedding day arrived. The aisle and altar were decorated with red and white roses and white babies' breath. The smell of fresh flowers filled the air as the roommates and I stood for Matt. He glowed, like a man in love, as Kim walked down the aisle where they said 'I do' to each other.

It was great to see so many friends again, it was almost a mini reunion of sorts. After the wedding ceremony was over, I saw Janet. She looked elegant in a simple, black short dress. Her hair was pulled back with a long, wispy piece draping her face, highlighting her beautiful eyes. She came to me and hugged me. I hoped she didn't notice that my heart was beating out of my chest as I hugged her back and asked her how her trip down had been.

We walked to the reception hall together. There were long tables with white linens, crystal glasses, and candles that made it a very warm and romantic setting. I was hoping for the relief of sitting on opposite sides of the room from Janet, so I could have time to collect myself. I went and sat next to Jason and Sandy as Janet visited with someone who approached her. I was thankful to be able to take a deep breath.

We visited for a while and then I made my way over to my table, only to find that Janet was seated right next to me. *Thanks a lot Matt; how am I going to handle this?* But I sat next to this beautiful woman and decided to enjoy our time together as *good friends.*

We started talking about everything as usual. We caught up since our last phone call, when she told me about some of her patients as an Occupational Therapist. She knew I was struggling with my business. She listened intently when I shared my concerns. I told her I decided to move in with Mark's parents for a while to figure things out and to save money. She thought that was a great idea, and asked about my place at the Schmidt's.

We had the best night. We listened to the beautiful music playing as Matt and Kim danced their first dance together as a couple, and cut the cake. A sense of calm came over me as I began to realize I was happy, just being close to her. It became even clearer to me that I just needed Janet in my life, even if it was only as a great friend.

After the ceremony was over, Janet and I continued enjoying our conversation. She wanted to see my place. So I took her over. The Schmidts were out of town, so we had the whole house to ourselves. We talked and laughed for hours. It was getting late and Janet had to

Photo of Stefan and Janet at Matt and Kim's wedding.
Photo from Stefan Bean's personal photo album, 1998.

get back to Fresno that next morning, so I took her up to see my room. She thought it was perfect and a great idea for me to be here.

She walked around my tiny space, commenting on my minimalistic decorating ability, which only included a USC poster and banner. She didn't speak; she just looked at me. Finally, Janet stood before me in that unforgettable black dress. The way it hugged her frame, elegant and understated, like her. Her lips carried a hint of red color, just enough to make it difficult for me to think of her as just a friend. Her brown hair was straight, perfectly styled. But it was her brown eyes that held me there–calm, knowing, and full of something unspoken.

She sat by me on the bed, then–without a word–she leaned in and kissed me. Softly, but with intention. Unmistakably real. *Is this really happening?* I asked myself with a stunned, yet elated, look on my face.

Eight long years of friendship, of almost and not quite, of waiting and wondering and walking through trials side by side. We held each other through losses, through uncertainty, through the kinds of moments that either break people apart or bind them together. And now–this kiss. Just when I had given up hope. The culmination of everything was unexpected. But in my soul, I knew it was meant to be. Like something sacred had finally found its place.

As she pulled away, she gave me a smile, not a casual grin, but *that* smile…the one that speaks without speaking. The one that told me, "This is it. This is the beginning of *us*."

The moment wasn't just romance. It was about timing, trust, and a truth we had both known but never dared to say out loud. It was the start of forever, disguised as a gentle kiss. Those eight years before that moment flashed before my eyes. *She did want to be with me. It just took her longer.* The conversations, the laughter, the difficult times when we were there for each other, and even the rejections were a necessary part of our journey, all leading to this perfect moment.

After years of waiting and rejection, I finally saw that even disappointment could become a doorway. What I thought was an ending became a beginning. It reminded me that potential often grows in the soil of struggle; and when someone believes in you, even in your lowest moments, it can ignite hope you didn't know you still carried.

> After years of waiting and rejection, I finally saw that even disappointment could become a doorway.

For once, I didn't have to ask her for a yes. I didn't have to ask if this was *something*. I didn't have to ask if she was ready yet. I knew without a word we were finally together. And she knew, too. I waited for her because she was the only one for me. My dream came true that night.

A week after the wedding, Janet and I couldn't wait any longer to see each other, so we met in Bakersfield at Eric and Sandy's house. What had once been long conversations between friends now felt different, deeper. We started talking every day, sometimes for six hours at a time, as if we were making up for all the years we had danced around what we both really wanted. At Eric and Sandy's, they smiled knowingly at the change they could sense in us, this time putting us in separate bedrooms to give space for what was quietly unfolding.

It was during one of these visits that Eric and Sandy suggested a simple outing—a picnic at the Kern River. It seemed ordinary enough, but in my heart I knew it would become something much more.

The day was radiant, with the sun warming the earth and a soft breeze moving gently through the trees. Janet spread the blanket with easy grace, her movements so familiar after years of friendship, yet now they stirred something entirely new in me. I hopped out of my wheelchair and sat beside her, and for a moment we just looked at each other, silently acknowledging that this was no longer just friendship.

As our lips met by the river, I felt years of doubt and longing begin to loosen their grip on me. The sting of teenage rejections, the crushes that faded, the girls who looked past me, the times I wondered if love would ever find me, was redeemed in that moment. It was all rewritten by the simple truth of her kiss. The warmth of the sun was nothing compared to the warmth I felt in my chest. The birds sang overhead, and the steady current of the river became the soundtrack to the beginning of something sacred.

Sandy and Janet had prepared a simple, but beautiful, picnic basket which included apples and grapes, turkey sandwiches, cheese and crackers, cookies for dessert. We picked at the food slowly, more interested in the company than the picnic. Hours slipped away as we talked, laughed, and kissed again and again, each one more certain than the last. It felt like our last "first date," and the beginning of forever disguised in the ordinary simplicity of a blanket by the river. For the first time, I stopped wondering if Janet and I would ever be. I knew we were.

Then I heard a cracking sound and looked over at my wheelchair that had been wedged behind a small rock. It started to roll down the hill to the riverbank faster than I could speak. I felt paralyzed physically and mentally at that moment when there was nothing I could do. My only mode of transportation splashed into the fast-rolling rapids of the Kern River and started to sink.

Out of the corner of my eye, Janet jumped up, quicker than anything I'd ever seen before. Without hesitation, she ran as fast as she could down the riverbank, jumped in the water just as the last surface of the wheelchair started to disappear. She grabbed it with all her might, lifted the chair out of the water and dragged it up the side of the riverbank back to safety. Only her desire to help me trumped her physical strength. She fully sacrificed herself at that moment for me, with no concern for being dragged to the bottom of the river by the strong current.

I experienced a flood of relief, slight embarrassment, and love wash over me all at once. I realized at that moment, *she will always take care of me. I need her forever.*

Getting back to Sandy and Eric's, they didn't believe our story, and thought we were teasing them. Janet was our evidence, being drenched from head to toe, that it really happened.

Our first date was amazing and memorable for sure. We continued visiting each other by train as often as we could. I would meet her parents and she would meet mine. So I took the train to visit Janet at her parent's farm, my first time meeting them and stepping into the world she grew up in. It was a humble, rural setting, far from anything I'd known, with the scent of damp earth and distant livestock hanging in the air.

As I walked in, the aroma of beans and rice, a staple in their Portuguese home, greeted me, quickly overtaken by the pungent, overwhelming smell of very fishy fish and sizzling blood sausage frying on the stove. Maria, her mom, was always in the kitchen. She shared her love through cooking for her family. Bowls and utensils covered every space on the kitchen counters.

I learned that when they lived in Portugal, Maria would kill a pig every year and feed the village. She knew how to prepare animals for a meal. I was able to see this firsthand once when we went fishing on the pier. A man started screaming, as he pulled up something that was trying to wiggle off his line. When he realized it was an octopus, he started to throw it back in, as he didn't quite know what to do with it. Maria stormed over to the octopus, planted one foot on its tentacles and turned its head inside out. She loads it on the butchering counter and starts chopping it up, all in a matter of minutes. She was a survivor who showed me where Janet got her strength.

Janet's dad was hard to get to know. He was tough, silent, and really didn't speak much, at least to me. At first, I thought it was because of his broken English, but later realized he just didn't want to speak that much to me. I wasn't afraid of him. I just wondered how we were ever going to build a relationship. His grumpiness actually changed for the better when he developed dementia later in his life. His personality completely changed; he became sweet and mild-mannered. While this was a good change, it was also sad.

When I walked into the kitchen, they both tried to feed me. I thought, *Great! Portuguese food sounds wonderful.* His mother served beans and rice. I was expecting some kind of meat or fish when her dad pulled something out of the refrigerator for me to try. I was intrigued until I saw it was still moving. I tried to keep my face calm, but inside I was panicking. *What in the world is that? Is it…still moving? There's no way I can eat this. How do I get out of this without insulting him?* My eyes darted to Janet, hoping she could read the look on my face. Sure enough, she jumped in before I had to say a word. "He can try that another time," she said with a smile and a little giggle, rescuing me in the smoothest way possible. I would later learn it was a rock limpet, a Portuguese sea snail that clings tightly to the coastal rocks.

Janet and I continued seeing each other as much as possible over the next year. She came with me to San Diego to meet my family. When Janet walked in, my mom and some of the kids were sitting in the living room, waiting for our arrival. I hugged my mom. She welcomed Janet with a hug and a few words. I could see she had a look of approval on her face already.

The kids took to Janet quickly. Especially Jasmine, my African American sister with cerebral palsy, who was intellectually disabled. Janet's work as an occupational therapist gave her much experience working with disabled children. Experience aside, Janet had a kindness and gentleness about her with an ability to know the needs of others. Her loving nature drew Jasmine in the minute she walked through the door. She went right to her and started playing with her and talking to her. My two brothers with Autism equally gravitated towards her. Janet enjoyed meeting my mom and siblings. She knew we'd have to travel elsewhere to meet my father.

My mom and dad decided to divorce when I was in my 20s, which was the biggest surprise to everyone who knew them. These two loving individuals who lived a life of sacrifice as one team, called it quits. It was shocking news for me and my siblings.

My parents were older now and my dad decided to retire right when my mom wanted to adopt Jared and Jordan #2. As much as my dad loved the boys, he was tired and wanted to travel and enjoy his hard-earned retirement. Adopting two more young boys meant fourteen more years of raising them, and that's exactly what my mom wanted to do. It was like starting all over again for my dad and he had reached his limit. Unfortunately, he put his foot down, but so did she. Janet and I would have to make two trips to see my parents, one to our old house, where my mom and the kids lived, and one to downtown San Diego where my dad lived now. So we planned it next time.

Fresno became our new hangout when Janet decided to move there for work. Our very first night, we were lying on the floor of her apartment, with the only light in the room coming from the moon that shone on her beautiful face. The soft glow poured through the window, casting gentle shadows across the floor. The world outside was quiet, the city hushed as if it, too, was holding its breath for what was coming.

Janet nestled into me, her head resting gently on my shoulder, the slow rhythm of her breathing syncing with mine.

I wrapped my arms around her, feeling the warmth of her body against mine. In that stillness, all the loneliness I had ever carried, from the streets of Saigon to the corners of every heartbreak, felt like it had finally come to rest. She tilted her head, looked up at me with eyes full of something I didn't quite have words for, and whispered, "I love you."

For a second, the world froze. The room held its breath. I felt my chest tighten, afraid to even move in case I'd imagined it. It was quiet. So quiet. But it felt louder than anything I'd ever heard. No one had ever said that to me with such sweetness, with such conviction. I had spent my whole life wondering if someone could ever see me fully through my disability and still choose me.

I didn't hesitate. The words flew out of my mouth before I could catch them, like a dam finally breaking. "I love you," I said, and I meant it with every fiber of who I was. It came out not like a confession, but like a burst of sunlight through clouds I'd lived under my whole life. It was raw. It was real. It was mine. In that moment, I knew I hadn't just survived life. I had found someone who would walk through it with me. I wasn't wondering anymore if I'd ever be loved. I was being loved. And I was loving right back.

My first visit to her new place included meeting her friends. Many of them worked with her. I could tell how much everyone loved her. She not only took care of the kids, but she also helped comfort and support their parents through challenging times.

She showed me albums of the children she worked with. Comfort, trust, love, and admiration beamed through the smiles on their faces as they posed for pictures with her. She showed me exactly what kind of mother she would be. I sighed heavily, knowing I could never have kids. How could I deprive Janet of something that was so natural, so import-ant to her? I snapped back to the moment when I recognized that I was getting way ahead of myself–or was I? I would ask Janet to marry me. Not having children was something we'd have to address, but not now. I decided to ask her dad for her hand in marriage.

Before I got back on the road, I told Janet I wanted to have one more meal with her parents, preferably a meal that was not alive. She laughed as we headed to the farm. It seemed normal for us to visit. It seemed we spent more time with her family than with mine.

Janet and her mom were in the kitchen cooking dinner together when I pulled Antonio aside. So far, his broken English had been a convenient barrier for him to speak to me as little as possible, but today I needed an answer.

We sat in the cozy living room filled with worn furniture and faded wallpaper. He looked at me differently with a serious look on my face. I said, "Antonio, I love your daughter and I would love to have your permission and blessing to marry her."

He sat very still for a few moments that seemed like decades to me, when he finally said, "What? Are you sure?"

This was not the reaction I expected, but I was resolved to ask for her hand in marriage. I said emphatically, "Yes, I'm sure."

He went on in a comical way, "She's a very strong little girl. She always argues with me. She will argue with you. Are you sure?"

I laughed and said, "Yes, I'm sure."

I knew what he was talking about. Janet was silent, but strong. Her calm and reserved nature could never be mistaken for weakness. She was strong-willed and opinionated, and that's just one of the things I loved about her. He said, "OK."

I laughed, and went home to start the planning. Janet once told me she wanted to be proposed to in public, which was surprising to me. I figured she meant being proposed to in front of her friends, as I could never see us on the screen at a baseball game. I planned a surprise birthday party in Fresno that doubled as a proposal. With help from her sisters, I even practiced asking in Portuguese.

The day had come. I told Janet to get ready, I would be taking her out for a birthday dinner. She asked what to wear and I told her to just put a dress on. She looked beautiful in her dress.

Every detail was perfect—until her father, with his uncanny timing, showed up with twelve dirty pigs that he had just bought, and tasked her with washing them. And being the dutiful daughter, Janet went and put on different clothes and started washing the pigs. My jaw dropped to the ground as I thought, *What is he doing? He knows about the surprise birthday party because, of course, he's invited. Or was it a joke?*

I couldn't figure it out. To this day, I wonder if he sensed my plan to propose and did this on purpose to delay the proposal, but nothing was going to stop me. Love has a way of overcoming even the muddiest obstacles.

Janet finished, went in, showered, and got dressed again, like it was nothing. We drove to Fresno and we were late. I secretly made a call to let them know we were running late because she was washing pigs.

I told Janet we needed to make a stop on the way to dinner. I guided her in the direction of the back gate where everyone yelled, "SUR-PRISE!" She smiled as she was greeted by family and friends in festive Hawaiian attire.

This was the moment I had been waiting for all my life. I practiced saying "Will you marry me?" in Portuguese with her sisters for weeks. I was ready. The DJ called us to the center of the stage, saying Stefan has a surprise for Janet. I was hoping she thought it was a birthday gift and wasn't wise to my plan just yet, but I could tell by the way she looked down at the floor she was expecting it.

When the moment finally arrived, I stood before her, heart racing, ready to pour my soul into a single question. Instead of saying, "Quer casar comigo?", I said, "Quer casar com o queijo?" I was hoping to charm her with a touch of romance. But nerves betrayed me, and what tumbled out was a jumbled, "Will you marry the cheese?"

Her Portuguese brother gave a smirk at my humorous attempt, but Janet, with her radiant grace, saw right through my blunder. Her eyes sparkled with understanding, and without a word, she leaned in, her lips meeting mine in a tender kiss that silenced the world around us. Then, in a whisper meant only for me, she breathed...

LIFTED Value: **Inspire Potential** When leaders recognize and cultivate their team's potential, they will see motivation grow, energy rise, and a deeper sense of ownership will take root.

Lifted Insight:

"After years of waiting and rejection, I finally saw that even disappointment could become a doorway. What I thought was an ending became a beginning. It reminded me that potential often grows in the soil of struggle; and when someone believes in you, even in your lowest moments, it can ignite hope you didn't know you still carried."

Leadership Reflection: How can you turn discouragement into inspiration for others who are watching you lead?

CHAPTER 9

～

Lifted by Love

"Yes!"

Janet's lips curled into the smile I had waited years to see, and she said the word that changed everything: yes. For a moment, I couldn't breathe. Then the rush hit me and I turned to our family and friends, my voice breaking with joy as I shouted, "She said yes!" The crowd erupted in cheers and applause that shook the room. This wasn't the kind of ovation I'd earned from a speech or a game. It was louder, deeper, more personal. It was the sound of our love being celebrated, the triumph of every long wait and every painful rejection erased in an instant.

I trembled as I slid the ring onto her finger, my hands unsteady with joy and relief. Her brown eyes met mine, glowing with warmth, and her faint smile said more than words ever could. For a moment the noise around us faded, and it felt like the world was holding its breath. When she looked down at the ring and then back up at me, there was a quiet certainty in her expression. I knew she wasn't just accepting a ring—she was accepting me, and the life we would build together.

When the ring slid onto her hand, the crowd surged forward. Her sisters hugged her, friends clapped behind me, and voices shouted, "Finally!" It felt like everyone had been waiting for this moment with us.

I called Mark and Eric and said, "She said yes!" Their shouts and laughter echoed like they were standing right there in the crowd, amplifying my joy. For the first time in my life, I felt completely lifted, not just by Janet's yes, but by the sea of love that surrounded us.

For the first time in my life, I felt completely lifted, not just by Janet's yes, but by the sea of love that surrounded us.

As the celebration swirled around us, my eyes fell back to Janet's hand. The ring sparkled in the light, catching the attention of everyone who came in close to hug us. People admired it, but for me it was not beauty. That ring carried a story, one that started long before this moment, and one that made saying yes feel even more sacred.

I had spent months wondering how I could possibly find a ring worthy of Janet, a woman whose life was marked by faith, quiet strength, and a kind of elegance that never needed to be announced. Every store I walked into felt overwhelming. Nothing seemed right for her. The ring had to be more than beautiful; it had to carry meaning.

When we designed Janet's ring, we used the diamonds my mom had saved for me. It wasn't flashy; instead, just simple, meaningful, and rooted in family love. Those stones carried more than beauty; they held a legacy of love, kindness, and family that I wanted to build my life upon with Janet.

Janet knew that story, and when it came time to design her ring, she wanted to honor my mom's hope as much as my love. She had her own eye for simplicity and grace, and she helped guide the design so it reflected both of us. She chose what she wanted, not something flashy or extravagant, but something that carried the magnitude of our moment. That was Janet's way.

Together we chose a trinity design. A single gold band held my mom's diamonds, surrounded by two platinum rings. The three parts spoke to the foundation of our marriage bound by God through faith, family, and love. When I looked at that ring, I didn't just see a piece of jewelry. I saw the beginning of our story, a promise that what we were building would last.

When the crowd finally began to settle and the night grew quiet, I found myself sitting with Janet, still holding her hand. The long wait, the rejections, the doubts—all of it finally felt so far away. A life with her lay ahead.

It was that clarity that gave me the courage to make some major changes in the year ahead. I decided to move up to Fresno to be close to Janet, and to save money for our wedding, I rented a small room from our church pastor. It wasn't glamorous, but every sacrifice felt worth it because it brought me closer to her and closer to the future we were building.

Leaving my business was hard, but with Janet beside me I knew my heart belonged in education. It was work that could change lives, not just make a living. That small voice grew louder: I was meant to be in education. At Cal State Fresno, I trained as a teacher, learning how to manage classrooms and connect with students. I even wrote a children's book as part of the program which was something I'd never imagined before.

Through that year in Fresno, Janet was my anchor. After long days of classes and lesson planning, we would meet up for dinner or spend hours just talking about everything: our childhoods, our dreams, our fears, and the kind of family we wanted to build. I would sometimes stop by her workplace. I quickly noticed why she was so respected. Janet was so good at her job. Her coworkers loved her, and the families she served spoke about her with such gratitude. Watching her interact with them made me fall even more in love with her. She was a servant at heart, always giving, always lifting others.

That engagement year was filled with memories. On New Year's Eve, as the world prepared to step into a new millennium, Janet and

I walked hand-in-hand through downtown Fresno. Surrounded by crowds, but lost in our own little world, I already knew we were one. The turning of the century felt like the turning of our story. Every past heartbreak had led me here, proving just how worth the wait this love was.

A piece of the new foundation for our lives together came from finally stepping into the career I was meant for. Thinking about helping kids brought me alive in a way I hadn't experienced before. Every day in class, whether I was in my books learning about theories or actually teaching in the classroom as a student teacher, I felt like I was becoming more of my authentic self. For the first time, my passion and my purpose were aligned; and it was clear to me that serving children was where God had been leading me all along.

But in the middle of that joy, another thought haunted me. As much as I loved the idea of pouring into the lives of children, I couldn't escape the reality that the doctors had told me I would never father a child of my own. Late at night, the fear crept in: *Am I asking Janet to give up the chance of becoming a mother? Am I taking away something sacred before we even begin our life together?*

My stomach turned every time the thought came. Eventually, I knew I had to face it head-on. One evening over dinner, I gathered the courage to bring it up. "Janet, you know the doctors told me I can't have kids, right?"

She looked at me steadily and said, "Yes, Stefan, I know."

My voice shook as I went on: "I feel like I'm depriving you of the most sacred part of being a woman." For a moment I held my breath, afraid she might agree.

Instead, she reached across the table and said with conviction, "Stefan, I'm inspired by the loving kindness of your parents. We can adopt and give a child the same chance you and your siblings were given."

Her words broke through my fear. I realized once again how blessed I was to have found the most wonderful woman in the world. For the first time, I let myself imagine a future that was not shaped by what I couldn't give, but by what we would create together.

Walking out of that restaurant together, I knew more than ever that I was marrying the right woman. Janet's words weren't just reassuring; they were a promise. They told me that whatever came, she would meet it with faith, kindness, and strength. That night became a cornerstone for me, the moment I stopped worrying whether we could make it and started trusting that we always would.

With that conversation, any lingering doubts disappeared. Janet had given me the greatest gift: the freedom to dream our future without fear. From that night on, our engagement became less about waiting and more about building. Every conversation turned to the life before us, and before long we were caught up in the whirlwind of wedding planning.

We started by visiting venues. A few farms were on our list at first, but my concern was that her dad could access dirty pigs easily, and I could just imagine one of them wandering through our ceremony. We laughed at the pig washing memory that happened before our engagement party.

Eventually, we chose the tennis and racquetball club in Fresno. It had wide green lawns, a sweeping view of the hillside, and just enough space to hold our family and friends without losing its charm. It was the perfect mix of large and intimate, simple and beautiful—just like Janet.

Choosing our wedding party came next, and it was not any easier. I couldn't imagine this day without Mark and Eric, so I asked them both to stand beside me as best men. Eric had always helped me know I was enough and be comfortable with who I was. Mark, on the other hand, challenged me to be the best me. He showed me to push toward the future that God had planned for me. Together, they had shaped me in ways I could never fully explain, so having them both by my side felt exactly right.

Janet faced the same dilemma with her two sisters, and chose them both to be maids of honor. She was so close to Lucy and Tricia, always sharing stories with me about how they laughed together, leaned on each other, and supported one another through every season of life. Their bond was deeply rooted in the closeness of her Portuguese family, and their presence on our wedding day was simply an extension of the lifelong love they'd always shared.

Our friends and family quickly rallied around us. Jason ("Bear"), Matt, and Martin joined as groomsmen, while Amber, Lisa, and Joanna, stood with Janet. Every "yes" from our friends felt like another affirmation that this marriage was meant to be. It was also a reflection of how deeply their friendships and mentorships had shaped and lifted my life, a testament to how far I had come from being an orphan with so little. Now, I was a man surrounded by people who believed in me and celebrated the love I had found.

Wedding day photo with Stefan and groomsmen.
Photo from Stefan Bean's personal photo library.

The air hung heavy and still, thick with the scent of lavender roses and freshly mown grass. I could hear the buzz of a thousand bees and the low murmur of our families, all waiting in the sweltering one hundred- and six-degree heat. The groomsmen glared at me as they stood at the altar looking handsome in double breasted, black tuxedos as the sweat trickled down their backs. But even the heat couldn't dim the light of this moment.

As I stood with the guys, I glanced around at the beautiful area where we would say our vows to love each other for better or worse. It was draped with gorgeous lavender roses that hung in the center, while purple bouquets framed the center aisle that the love of my life would walk down. Janet's sisters and her girlfriends were in their lovely pastel-colored bridesmaid's dresses, looking much cooler than the guys.

Welling up with emotion, I tried to restrain myself from losing it too early, as Heidi came up front to sing a beautiful solo. Our families were there, seated in the front row looking sharp, as they were about to let one of us go, and welcome the other into the family. Luckily Antonio didn't show up with pigs to wash today, I thought to myself with a chuckle. My dad was quiet, but I could tell underneath he was emotional, as he put his arm around my sister to comfort her. Even through her tears, my mom had a profound glow of happiness that peered from underneath, creating confusion as to whether they were tears of joy or tears of sadness.

The music began and everyone rose. The moment Janet stepped into the sunlight and began walking down the aisle, the world seemed to pause. The heat, the sweat, the discomfort, all of it vanished in her glow. I looked at her from head to toe with a lump in my throat, realizing that every prayer I had whispered as a boy was answered in this single, breathtaking moment. Janet was the promise I never thought I would receive. And somehow, she was mine.

Her silky black hair, tousled in wispy curls, framed the glow of her face. She looked stunning in a satin gown with a lace overlay that draped her elegant curves. A classic round collar was knotted as it fell down the middle of her back against her smooth skin. Her bouquet of purple roses polished the look of the most beautiful bride I had ever seen. Her smile lit something eternal in me, and her eyes, so alive and so sure, told me the same: you are mine, and I am yours. Just as I wept then, I feel the tears even now, not from sorrow, but from a joy so pure it split me wide open. When she finally reached me, I smiled like I never had before. I knew in that instant that God had not only heard my prayers. He had given me more than I ever dared dream.

We spoke the vows we had written ourselves, promises shaped not only by our love but by the lives we had already lived. I told Janet I would cherish her in both laughter and sorrow, in health and in weakness, and that no matter what trials came, I would never let go of her hand. She promised to stand beside me, to lift me when I fell, and to trust God with every step of our journey. At the time, those words felt like poetry, the kind of vows every couple makes at the altar. Neither of us could have known how much those promises would be tested, or how deeply they would bind us together.

One hundred twenty-five family and friends lifted us up in prayer for our new life as husband and wife. In the years to come, I would look back on that moment and realize how those prayers did more than bless our beginning—they carried us through both the joys we celebrated and the storms we never imagined would come.

Cheers erupted when we walked back down the aisle as Mr. and Mrs. Bean. The ceremony flowed into an unforgettable celebration, filled with laughter, stories, and the kind of joy you wish you could bottle up and keep forever. Mark, in his toast, dug up some of my most embarrassing college moments and had everyone roaring with laughter, before turning serious and thanking Janet for finally taking me off his hands. Her sisters spoke with tenderness, painting a picture of Janet that reminded me how lucky I was to now call her my wife.

Photo of Janet on the wedding day.
Photo from Stefan Bean's personal photo album.

When it came time for our first dance, Janet and I smiled at each other knowingly. We had practiced for weeks, determined to make it something special. We moved together slowly, savoring the moment, and just as we planned, the dance ended with her settling gently in my lap, followed by a slight dip for a kiss. The room erupted in cheers.

It was great to see the dance floor filled with our closest friends and family, many of them dancing with their children. There was something beautiful about watching the people who had carried us, lifted us, and prayed for us, all gathered in one place to celebrate the start of our new life.

Janet's dad, Antonio, stood quietly off to the side for much of the night, but later he offered a simple, heartfelt speech. His words were brief but full of love, a father's blessing over his daughter and her new husband. Her mom, holding back tears, expressed her joy at seeing Janet so happy. I will never forget their faces at that moment.

At one point I found myself sitting across from my mentor, Bill Sanderson. I leaned in and told him how much his guidance had meant to me, how his mentorship had shaped not only my career but the man I had become. He smiled and told me he was proud of me, and that this was just the beginning.

Even the details that went "wrong" made the day sweeter. Our cake, decorated with purple and green grapes, began to melt in the heat before the knife ever touched it. But when we cut into it, the buttercream was rich and the strawberry filling burst with flavor, proof that even in a mess there was sweetness. Nothing could stop us now, we were *Mr. and Mrs. Bean.*

Photo of Stefan and Janet sharing wedding cake bites.
Photo from Stefan Bean's personal photo album.

After the reception ended and the laughter quieted, Janet and I slipped away to Old Town Hanford, where we had booked a night at a charming Victorian-style hotel, the kind of place where time seemed to stand still. The room was softly lit as the two of us entered the room, no crowd, no planning, no speeches—just us and the promise we sealed at the altar.

That night, our love was sealed in the deepest way. I will never forget the gentleness of her touch, the way she looked at me as if every scar, every imperfection, every trace of my journey was beautiful to her. I had always been self-conscious about my skinny legs, the visible marks left by my disability, but in her arms I felt nothing but acceptance. Janet's love reached deeper than appearance. Her eyes and her embrace told me that she saw all of me, and she chose all of me. Janet reminded me that authenticity is not about hiding imperfections. Instead, it's about being seen and still being embraced. I learned when we allow others to bring their whole selves, strengths and struggles together, trust takes root.

It was tender, it was full of laughter and wonder, and it was perfect. That night was not about passion alone, it was about trust, about finding in one another the safe place we had both been searching for. As we fell asleep in each other's arms, I knew this was the beginning of something lasting and beautiful, a love that would only grow deeper with time.

The morning after our wedding, still buzzing with joy and a little worn out from the heat and the celebration, we packed our bags and boarded a cruise ship bound for Mexico. We were exhausted from the heat and the hecticness of the wedding, but there was an energy between us that no amount of sun or sleeplessness could dim.

The ship became our little escape. We laughed through late dinners, lingered over endless buffets, and sat side by side at the evening shows. To be honest, we missed more shows than we made, because most evenings we simply stayed in our room together, savoring the sweetness of being newly married. Those quiet nights, away from the passengers, felt like the true highlight of the trip.

Occasionally when we came out of isolation, we dined with another newlywed couple we met on the ship. We instantly bonded with them through conversations about our journeys leading up to both wedding days. It was obvious that everyone noticed how beautiful Janet looked under the soft yellow lights. Their admiration made me smile and puff out my chest a bit. *Yes, she was all mine.*

Even the excursions, not always wheelchair friendly, turned into memories we would never forget. When it came time to take the tender boat to shore, Janet jumped in the water without hesitation, steadying me and my chair. She had a calm confidence about her that left me in awe. On the beach, she pushed me across the sand, as if she had been doing it her whole life. We spent the day laughing, swimming, and soaking in the joy of being newly married. Nothing could have been sweeter.

In Acapulco, the sidewalks had curbs so high they looked like small walls. As soon as locals saw me struggling to navigate, they rushed over without hesitation, lifting me up onto the sidewalk; their kindness was touching. Janet, who spoke three languages fluently, thanked them in Spanish with kind words only meant for them.

Returning home, the joyful memories of our cruise felt like the perfect foundation for our marriage. Filled with laughter and moments of unexpected kindness, it left us with a powerful sense that, together, we could face any obstacle.

Before the wedding, I had graduated and accepted a teaching position in Long Beach. The school was in a very poor area, and the challenges were unlike any I had faced before. Still, I felt grateful. The work made me grow as a leader by presenting me with sometimes insurmountable obstacles. I was placed where I was needed, and I would fight for these kids every day.

Janet and I settled into our first home together, a small one-bedroom condo in Belmont Heights. Life was simple. We didn't have much furniture, just a mattress and a table we made on the floor; none of that mattered. We sat together, surrounded by gifts. The flatware, dishes, and pots were more than just ordinary household items; they were the vessels for the meals we would cook and share for years to come.

The walking distance from our Second Street condo to the beach would become part of the rhythm of our marriage. We spent countless evenings strolling down to the shore or into town, eating at little restaurants, laughing, and talking about everything from our day-to-day lives to the dreams we had for our future. Those simple walks and dinners weren't extravagant, but they became the heartbeat of our early marriage. They gave us the chance to slow down, to learn about each other more deeply, and to grow into the life we were building side by side.

At the same time, we knew we needed to plant roots in a faith community. Janet's heart especially longed for the stability and fellowship of a church family. We found our home at Bethany Church, where we attended Sunday services, joined Bible studies, and shared meals at potluck dinners that felt more like family gatherings than informal events. Friendships grew quickly. People welcomed us not just as a young couple but as partners in faith, and Janet's warmth drew others to her almost immediately.

Those evenings we'd host Bible study, filled with laughter, prayer, and honest conversation, gave us a sense of belonging that turned our little condo into a true home. Our marriage was no longer just the two of us. It was also about the community that surrounded us, encouraged us, and reminded us that faith would be the foundation for everything we would build together. At the time, it felt like a blessing of fellowship. Only later would we realize how important our circle of faith was to lift us up when life became more than we could bare alone.

We quickly settled into a routine as our first year of marriage unfolded. I spent my days teaching in Long Beach, often coming home with a stack of papers to grade and stories of students whose behaviors tested me daily. Janet was working as an occupational therapist, and more than once she offered suggestions for how I might handle the most troubled kids. Her insight was steadying, and her faith was a constant reminder to me of why I had chosen this path.

Evenings were simple but meaningful. We shared dinners at home, often something Janet prepared with her quiet touch of care, then we would head out for walks together through Belmont Heights or down to the beach. Weekends meant church, Bible study, and time with our growing circle of friends. Life was full, but it was also steady, marked by a rhythm that carried us through those early months together.

When our first anniversary arrived, we celebrated with a meal at Open Sesame, a Mediterranean restaurant that quickly became a favorite of ours. We would return there often, savoring the flavors and the memories of those first twelve months together. That tradition began in those early days, a reminder that while the year passed in a blur, the love we were building was only getting stronger.

One evening Janet decided to cook a Portuguese meal, wanting to share a piece of her family's tradition with me. She started with Caldo Verde, a hearty soup made with kale, potatoes, and Portuguese sausage, then brought out sea bass drizzled with olive oil. I teased her that I was just grateful she knew better than to serve me anything still alive. She rolled her eyes and laughed, but her smile told me she loved my silly relief.

We lingered over dessert, a simple plate of fruit and cheese, when Janet slid a small white box across the table. Her expression was playful, almost mischievous. I raised an eyebrow, not sure what to expect. Inside was a thermometer. I pulled it out, turning it over in my hands with a puzzled look. *A thermometer? Why would she give me this? Is she sick? Did I miss something?* "A thermometer? You're not sick, are you?" I asked.

Janet giggled and shook her head. "No, Babe…we're going to have a baby."

LIFTED Value: **Foster Authenticity** Leadership should never be about appearances or titles. It has to be about living honestly, scars and all, and allowing others to see that grief and strength can live side by side.

Lifted Insight:

"I had always been self-conscious about my skinny legs, the visible marks left by my disability, but in her arms I felt nothing but acceptance. Janet's love reached deeper than appearance. Her eyes and her embrace told me that she saw all of me, and she chose all of me. Janet reminded me that authenticity is not about hiding imperfections. Instead, it's about being seen and still being embraced. I learned when we allow others to bring their whole selves, strengths and struggles together, trust takes root."

Leadership Reflection: What parts of your own journey or imperfections, if shared, could build deeper trust with others?

CHAPTER 10

The Unwritten Path: Lifted by Life

For a moment, the world stopped, my mind going blank and racing all at once. It wasn't possible; not one, not two, but several doctors had told me this could never happen. *Did I hear her right? Did she really just say we're having a baby?*

I stared at her, then at the thermometer, then back at her. "What? No way."

She burst out laughing at my wide-eyed disbelief, and I couldn't help but laugh, too. My face must have gone pale because she reached across the table and touched my hand, steadying me. Slowly, the truth sank in.

The weeks that followed were full of wonder and adjustment. Janet handled the pregnancy with her usual grace, but that didn't mean it was easy. Morning sickness became her constant companion, and though it usually passed by midday, I could see how much it took out of her. I tried to help where I could—fetching ginger ale, bringing watermelon, keeping things light with jokes that she didn't appreciate. Most of all, I just marveled at her resilience.

Our friends and family were overjoyed, and their excitement seemed to grow with every passing month. Janet glowed, and everyone wanted to be part of the celebration. At her baby shower, I was included, which meant more to me than I could put into words. Sitting there surrounded by gifts, laughter, and prayers for our little one, I realized just how supported we were.

One of the highlights was choosing the crib. We wanted it to be safe, sturdy, and something that would last, so we chose one carefully. When the big box finally arrived, I took charge of assembling it. Piece by piece, I tightened bolts, lined up slats, and followed instructions as best I could. By the time I was done, I stepped back with pride, grinning at Janet. She smiled and teased, "Let's just hope it holds together."

Through it all, our excitement grew with each ultrasound. Seeing the image of our baby girl on the screen gave us a sense of peace that our baby was healthy and developing normally; each kick and each doctor's visit was another step toward our blessing of becoming parents. The anticipation filled our little condo as Janet continued cleaning and organizing. It was no longer just the space we lived in, it was a nest, waiting for the life we were about to welcome.

As the months rolled by, anticipation gave way to restlessness. The due date came and went, but still no baby. Janet remained calm, far calmer than I was, and insisted we carry on with life as usual. One evening, more than a week past her due date, she suggested we go out for a nice dinner in Newport Beach.

We walked together up a steep hill toward the restaurant, the salty air of the ocean mixing with the aroma of food from the kitchens around us. I remember watching in amazement as Janet, carrying a full-term baby, pushed herself up the hill with ease, her strength and determination on full display. By the time we reached the top, both of us joked that hopefully the climb might do the trick.

Sure enough, a few days later, the contractions began. I was at work when she called, her voice calm though her breathing told me it was real. "Stefan, it's time," she said. Her voice was a calm whisper that cut through the noise of my racing heart. She was ready and this was it.

I drove gently, passing shops and restaurants at a crawl, not wanting to jar her or the baby in any way. Janet later teased me that I drove like an old man. The drive to the hospital felt like it lasted forever but eventually we made it. Janet's contractions grew stronger, and soon the delivery room was filled with moaning and the sound of rhythmic breathing. An epidural was offered more than once, but Janet shook her head each time. She wanted our baby to start life free of interventions, even if it meant bearing the pain herself.

Five and a half hours later, with a cry that split the silence, our daughter, Sophia Arianna Bean, entered the world. She was born in the fall of 2002, and in that moment, every fear and doubt I had carried was replaced with awe. Looking at Janet as she cradled our little girl with tears streaming down her cheeks, was the most beautiful sight I'd ever seen. I sat beside her, overwhelmed, whispering prayers of thanks, I was filled with an immense gratitude that words couldn't describe.

When the nurse finally placed Sophia in my arms, my whole body tensed. I had held many babies before, growing up in a house filled with foster children, each one needing love and care. But this was different. I was in awe at the miracle of birth, but not just any miracle—our miracle. This was not a child I would love for a season and then say goodbye to. This was my daughter, my own flesh and blood, and the magnitude of that truth made my hands shake.

Her tiny fingers curled instinctively around mine; her face, delicate and peaceful, made my heart pound as I prayed I would be the father she needed. I whispered her name softly, barely able to speak, as tears blurred my vision. *This was my daughter. Thank you, God.*

We named her Sophia, which means wisdom, a name that fit her perfectly. Even as a baby, looking into her eyes, I could sense a depth that told me she would achieve great things in her life. As the years

Photo of Sophia, Janet God's gift from heaven.
Photo from Stefan Bean's personal photo album, 2002.

passed, it would come to describe the deeply intelligent young woman she grew to be. Just like her mom, Sophia developed the will, the drive, and the heart to carry out any mission placed before her.

Janet chose to stay home with Sophia during those first years, and it was one of the greatest gifts she could give our family. She poured herself into motherhood with the same grace and dedication she brought to every part of her life. When I came home from teaching during that time, I'd find her rocking Sophia in her arms, singing softly, or laughing as our daughter reached out with curious little hands. Tired, and often with a stack of papers to grade, Sophia's giggle or the sight of Janet's smile gave me the energy to keep going. Having my family at home gave me permission to focus on teaching others.

Teaching was deeply fulfilling. I learned quickly that students needed more than lessons; they needed patience, structure, and someone to believe in them. I wanted to be someone who made a difference to everyone. Now, as a parent, I appreciated the trust parents placed in me to teach and care for their child.

Our home was small, but it was filled with love. Nights were often spent talking with Janet after Sophia fell asleep. Contentment hardly described it, as we marveled at our unexpected blessings. I finally had a wife I adored, a daughter who changed my life, and a career that clearly defined my purpose. For the first time, I felt every part of my life was aligned.

Soon after Sophia was born, my career took a surprising turn. I was invited to attend a teaching conference where I stopped at a table for an education company out of Johns Hopkins University. They were hiring literacy consultants, and before I knew it, I had been offered the job. It was an opportunity I hadn't expected, but it felt like a natural step forward.

The work allowed me to travel, to step into schools and work directly with educators on reading and literacy. Standing in front of large groups of teachers, I realized just how much I loved presenting and how naturally it came to me. What had once been practice in classrooms with students became practice in conference rooms and auditoriums with adults. The purpose was the same: to lift others so they could lift their students.

I absolutely loved it. Speaking to educators about the strategies and systems that could transform classrooms gave me an energy I hadn't felt before. It was a natural progression from teaching children, to teaching adults how to reach children. Each presentation sharpened my skills and gave me a sense that my platform and my responsibility was growing. Looking back, that season taught me more than just how to teach literacy. It shaped me as a leader.

The large conference room buzzed with the energy of educators and leaders. Conversations, fueled by coffee and croissants, swirled around the round tables, a vibrant soundscape of people united by a single purpose: to help children.

Chills ran up my spine as I walked on stage that day. I felt authentic, like I had finally stepped into me. I learned the importance of lifting others by giving them tools to do the work they were called to do; encouragement to break through the barriers that were holding them back, and belief in their own capacity to change lives. I could feel their acceptance and their genuine interest in hearing what I had to say.

It was my first glimpse of what would later become a cornerstone of my leadership framework. Leadership is not about being the expert in the room, but about empowering others to rise to reach their potential. My purpose was clear and I was on my way.

Sophia was just over a year old when I noticed a small lump beneath my ear, near the side of my neck. At first, I brushed it off as nothing more than a swollen gland. Life was busy, and with Janet, Sophia, and my new role with Johns Hopkins, it was easy to push my own health aside.

It wasn't until a family camping trip that Robert, a friend who was also a doctor, pulled me aside and said, "Stefan, you really need to get that checked." His concern unsettled me. When we arrived home, I finally made the appointment.

The diagnosis came back as a Schwannoma tumor, a benign peripheral nerve tumor. The word "benign" brought me some comfort, but the doctors explained that its location was complicated. It was growing directly out of a nerve near my face and was wrapped around my facial nerves. It needed to come out, but the risks were high.

I thought this surgery would be minor. I was wrong. The doctors cut through my main facial nerve, and I woke up paralyzed on the left side of my face. My smile was gone. To reach the tumor, they chiseled around my eardrum, leaving me with crushing vertigo. The room spun, nausea consumed me, and no one could tell me when it would stop.

For the first time in our marriage, Janet and I were faced with a trial that tested everything we had promised at the altar. We had spoken words about loving each other in sickness and in health, in joy and in sorrow, and now those vows were no longer poetry. They were our reality.

Mark and Janet came to the hospital to bring me home. As I tried to steady myself in the car, Mark pulled out a pillow from nowhere and tucked it gently in front of my head. I lay against it on the dashboard, too dizzy to hold myself upright, while he drove slowly and kept checking on me. Janet had worked hard to make our apartment ready, scrubbing it clean and washing all the bedding so I would be comfortable. But when I walked through the door, the scent of detergent sent me reeling. Without hesitation, she stripped the bed and rewashed everything in plain water, determined to make the space bearable for me. In that moment, Mark's quiet friendship and Janet's devotion lifted me when I could not lift myself.

Those first days at home were some of the hardest of my life. I barely spoke. I hardly ate. Laughter felt impossible. Sophia, with her bright, innocent eyes, would toddle over to me holding out a toy, her little giggle echoing in the silence. I wanted so badly to smile back, but the left side of my face would not move. The smile I longed to give her stayed trapped inside. I felt like a stranger in my own body, unable to connect with the very people who were my everything.

Janet never wavered. She prayed with me, talked to me, and pushed me even when I resisted. "Come on, Stefan, up and down," she would say as she helped me move, refusing to let me give in to despair. Her faith was steady when mine faltered. She carried enough determination for both of us. Her love for me was fierce, faithful and forever.

The days dragged on, and with them came waves of discouragement. I sat for hours in silence, the room spinning, my body betraying me. I barely touched food, and conversations felt impossible. I hated that Sophia's laughter, which had once filled me with joy, now made me ache because I couldn't respond the way I wanted. Depression settled in like a fog, and even I barely recognized myself.

Janet, though, refused to give up. She prayed aloud over me when I couldn't find the words. She reminded me that I was still the man she loved, even if I felt broken. She coaxed me to move, even when every step made my head spin. Her love was not fragile. It was strong, relentless, and determined enough for both of us.

Slowly, progress began to show: I could blink again without the small weight the doctors had placed on my eyelid. Then my speech started to clear. I had to work harder, focusing on each sound, but in the struggle, I became a stronger speaker, paying more attention to projection and articulation. What felt like a cruel setback was, in time, sharpening one of the very gifts God had given me.

Still, there were losses I grieved quietly. My boyish smile was gone, replaced by an unfamiliar face in the mirror. I could no longer whistle, something so small but so woven into how I expressed joy. And behind my ear, another scar had been added to the collection, one more visible reminder of the battles my body had endured. Yet with Janet by my side, the vertigo lessened, the fog lifted, and little by little, I began to feel like myself again. I had not chosen these scars, but I was learning that resilience could be its own kind of beauty.

By the time I began to feel more like myself again, life was moving forward in ways I had once feared I would never see. At work, my role was expanding as I partnered with principals, helping them analyze data, shape instruction, and lead their teams with clarity. I realized that leadership was not just about vision, but about equipping others to succeed. Even as I carried a new scar and the reminder of what I had lost, I found purpose in helping others discover what was possible.

So when Janet planned a celebratory dinner for my birthday, it felt like more than just a milestone. It was about survival, healing and entering a new chapter. Janet went all out for my birthday that year. She cooked one of my favorite meals, set the table with candles, and carried herself with a quiet excitement I couldn't quite place. After dinner, she brought out a small gift box wrapped neatly in white paper.

I opened it slowly, expecting maybe a watch or something sentimental. Inside was another thermometer. *I know what this means.* I looked at her, speechless, my mouth opening but no words coming out. She smiled, that playful smile that said she knew she had me exactly where she wanted me. "Stefan," she said softly, "you know what this means." Then the tears came for both of us as the joyfulness sank in again. Our love was the improbable author of a new chapter–a reward that rewrote a story we thought was already written.

The months before Amelia's birth were filled with a mix of excitement and nerves. Sophia, still so little herself, didn't quite understand what it meant to become a big sister, but she seemed to sense something important was coming. She would scooch over to Janet's growing belly and rest her hand there, giggling when she felt the baby move.

As Amelia's due date drew near, the doctors prepared us for the possibility of a C-section because she was breech. We prayed often during those weeks, asking God to guide the delivery and protect both Janet and the baby. Then, just in time, Amelia turned on her own, and Janet's strength and determination carried her once again.

Labor was long and intense. Eleven hours of pain, pushing Janet to her limits, yet she refused to take an epidural, just as she had with Sophia. Her faith and her fierce love for our child gave her the strength to keep going. I stood at her side, nervous, helpless at times, but filled with awe at the grit and grace she showed in every contraction.

Then came the moment that nearly stopped my heart. Amelia was born silent, her face tinged purple, the cord wrapped around her neck. Terror surged through me as the doctors worked to free her. The room fell into a silence that felt like hours, though only seconds passed. I wanted to breathe for her but could not find my own breath. Then, with a gasp and a cry, her voice filled the air. The sound released the room and sent tears streaming down my face.

In the winter of 2005, Amelia Julianna Bean was born. I looked at Janet, exhausted but radiant, and then at our new daughter, so tiny yet so fierce in her arrival. Together, we exhaled, overwhelmed with gratitude that Amelia came safely into the world.

When we brought Amelia home, it wasn't just an ordinary homecoming. We wanted Sophia to feel celebrated too, so we threw her a "Big Sister Party." Family and friends gathered, bringing little gifts just for her—dolls, books, and outfits labeled "Big Sis." Sophia beamed with pride as she held her baby sister in her lap, even if only for a few seconds at a time. Watching her step into that new role reminded me how quickly our little girl was growing, and how our family was stepping into a brand-new chapter together. I enjoyed my time off with the girls, helping everyone settle into our ever-changing life together, but I had to get back to work.

My work was winding down. I had loved my role as a consultant, traveling and helping schools strengthen literacy, but I was presented with a great opportunity. I was being recruited to serve as principal at my very own school in South Los Angeles. It was a community that faced enormous challenges, but it was also filled with students who needed someone to believe in them, like me. The thought of leading an entire school—not just influencing teachers but shaping the culture of a campus—stirred something in me. It was daunting and exhilarating, and I knew it was the next step.

As our little family grew to four, so did my sense of responsibility, both at home and in my calling. Each morning I looked at Janet, Sophia, and Amelia, and I knew I wasn't just working for myself anymore. I was working to lift them up, provide and lead with a heart shaped by the love we were building together.

Entering my first year as principal in South Los Angeles was thrilling and overwhelming. The school was full of students who had so much potential, but the burden of poverty, trauma, and low expectations pressed heavily on the community. I came in eager to make a difference, determined to raise student achievement from the start. But no matter how hard I pushed on academics, the results weren't there. Test scores hardly moved, and some even dropped.

The frustration grew heavier with each passing month. I worked long hours, tried every strategy I knew, and still felt like I was coming up short. Late at night I would sit at my desk, asking myself what I was missing. I wanted to believe in my vision, but I couldn't escape the sense that something fundamental was out of place.

It wasn't until my second year that the realization began to sink in. Achievement doesn't rise in a vacuum. You cannot demand performance without first creating an environment where teachers feel supported, students feel seen, and families feel valued. I had been so focused on test scores that I had overlooked the foundation that made those scores possible: culture.

So I shifted. I started by listening more—to teachers, to parents, and especially to students. I celebrated small wins. I made sure people felt heard. I began shaping traditions that made students proud to belong to our school. It wasn't glamorous work, and it didn't show up on data charts right away. But it was real. Slowly, trust began to grow.

It took two full years of steady work before I saw the tide begin to turn. By my fourth year, the results started to speak for themselves. Test scores rose, students showed greater confidence, and teachers embraced new strategies with energy. I realized that leadership wasn't about quick fixes or pushing harder. It was about building culture—a community of belonging and belief—and then watching academics rise as a result. That lesson became one of the anchors of my leadership journey. Real change doesn't begin with numbers. It begins with people.

While the school stretched me in every way, home grounded me. No matter how long or difficult the day had been, walking through the door to Sophia's laughter and Amelia's tiny hands reaching for me made everything else fade into the background.

Janet was the steady center of our family. She poured herself into raising our girls with patience and creativity, filling their days with stories, play, and faith. I would often come home late, drained from trying to turn around a struggling school, but the sight of Janet on the floor with the girls, building block towers or reading picture books, reminded me of what truly mattered.

We found joy in the simplest things. Weekend walks, shared meals, bedtime routines where we sang songs and prayed together. The condo that once felt small for just the two of us now seemed alive with giggles, toys scattered across the floor, and the sweet chaos of early parenthood.

In the middle of my struggle to build culture at school, I realized that Janet and I were building our own culture at home—one of love, laughter, and faith. It gave me perspective. I was determined to help students who didn't come from the kind of home I had.

Our house was warm and full, with Sophia and Amelia filling our days with joy. But soon they began asking for something more. "We want a brother," they would tell Janet with wide eyes. Janet gently explained that this wasn't something we could control. "If you want a baby brother," she told them, "you'll need to pray."

Sophia took her mom at her word. Every morning she would climb out of bed, fold her little hands, and pray the same prayer with childlike sincerity: "Dear God, please bring me a little brother. I promise to look after him. Thank you."

One afternoon, Janet had quietly taken a pregnancy test but hadn't yet shared the results. As she sat on the bed, still holding the secret close, Sophia climbed up beside her, placed a hand on her stomach, and said with confidence, "Mom, God answered my prayer. He told me we're going to have a baby brother." Janet froze, her eyes wide, and then, with tears welling, she whispered to herself, *This is God.*

Weeks later, the ultrasound confirmed what Sophia already knew. We were having a boy. In the summer of 2007, after eleven long hours of labor, Samuel Mark Nam Bean was born—a firecracker baby with a name rooted in the verse from 1 Samuel 1:27: *"For this child I prayed, and the Lord has granted me my petition which I asked of Him."* From the very beginning, Samuel's life was a testament to the little kid's faith.

Our condo suddenly seemed to shrink with toys scattered in every corner, baby gear filling the rooms, and the constant hum of little voices. Exhausted, Janet moved with grace through it all, somehow managing feedings, naps, and playtime while still keeping our home a place of warmth and peace.

I was deep into my master's program during this season, often staying up late at night with textbooks and papers spread across the table after the kids were asleep. There were times when the pressures of school, work, and fatherhood felt like too much, but every time I looked at Janet holding our children or saw Sophia and Amelia playing together with Samuel nearby, I knew why I was doing it. Each sacrifice was for them.

Our friendships also deepened in these years. Mike and Amber Post became like family, their four kids growing up side by side with ours. We laughed together over the chaos of parenting, leaned on each other for support, and shared countless meals where the kids spilled as much food as they ate. Around the same time, Sean and Beckie Daley entered our lives. Their family eventually grew to eight children, but in those early years, our kids were inseparable. We spent weekends together, swapped babysitting, and built a community that felt as essential as oxygen.

Janet and I stepped more intentionally into mentoring young families. We remembered how mentors had lifted us in our early days and wanted to do the same for others. Our living room was often filled with couples talking about marriage, faith, and parenting while little ones ran through the halls. It wasn't polished, but it was real, a reminder that God never meant us to do life alone. At the time, we saw it as the gift of community. We didn't yet know it would become a lifeline in the darkest days ahead.

By the time Samuel was a toddler, Janet and I were convinced our family was complete. Soon after, God gave us *His* own answer.

For my birthday in 2010, Janet and the kids surprised me with a trip to Disneyland. It was already the perfect gift—a weekend filled with magic and laughter. At breakfast, as I unwrapped presents from the girls, Sophia and Amelia started giggling uncontrollably. I opened a package and pulled out a tiny Mickey Mouse baby jumper. "How cool," I said, "where did you find this?" I looked up to see Janet smiling with tears in her eyes.

She leaned across the table and said the words that once again left me speechless: "Stefan, we're having another baby."

The girls squealed, Samuel banged his spoon on the table in celebration, and I sat there stunned, laughing and crying all at once. Gabriella would arrive later that year, she would be the missing piece of our family, completing us in ways we didn't even know we needed.

Rapidly entering the hospital, Gabriella was coming quickly. By then, the nurses were used to Janet politely but firmly refusing an epidural, just as she had with every birth before. They would glance at each other, shake their heads, and say nothing more. I would never know the pain of childbirth, but I knew where Janet's toughness came from, her Portuguese mother. Grit was passed down through generations, and it carried her through every contraction as she finally pushed Gabriella into the world. In those hours Janet's strength was enough to bring new life into the world, but eventually it would be called upon to hold onto life itself. From the moment she was placed in our arms. The Bean family was complete.

The older kids crowded around to meet their baby sister. Sophia, proud as ever, leaned in gently as if to check whether her prayers still worked, while Amelia giggled and announced to anyone listening, "I'm a big sister, too!" Samuel, still so little himself, stood wide-eyed, fascinated by the tiny bundle of blankets and pink cheeks.

Photo of Amelia, Sophia, Gaby and Samuel.
Photo from Stefan Bean's personal photo library.

For me, holding Gabriella was a mixture of awe and relief. After all the surprises and setbacks of life, here was another gift I never expected. I traced her tiny fingers with my own and felt the gravity of what it meant to be the father of four.

Janet had this way of being tough when she needed to be, the Portuguese fire she carried, but tender when it mattered most. Our kids always knew that Mom could fix it, whether it was a scraped knee, a broken toy, or a broken heart. I knew in those moments I had married the perfect woman for me and our children. She made our house a place where love wasn't just spoken, it was lived every day.

That same year, I stepped into my second principal assignment and earned my master's degree in organizational leadership. It was the hardest professional year of my life. I was handed a leadership team that didn't share my vision for the school, and instead of walking with me, they resisted and undermined me at nearly every turn. The frustration was relentless. It took me nearly a year to realize that the problem wasn't only their resistance—it was also my failure to communicate clearly. I had not yet learned how to bring others along, to reach both their hearts and minds while laying out a path forward. That painful year taught me that vision unspoken is vision wasted, and leadership requires more than drive. It requires clarity, patience, and trust.

Life with our little tribe was a beautiful kind of chaos that I was always ready to come home to. Our condo was filled with the sound of laughter, cries, singing, and the thud of little feet racing across the floor. No matter how long the day had been, those closing minutes at bedtime like reading to the kids,

> Life with our little tribe was a beautiful kind of chaos that I was always ready to come home to.

wrapped everything in peace. It felt like we had finally reached the summit we had been climbing toward for years and I had been climbing my whole life. There was always a too-good-to-be-true moment in the back of my mind: *How long would this wonderful feeling last?*

One winter, we caravanned to the mountains with our closest friends the Posts and the Daileys. The roads were slick with snow and fog, but when we finally arrived, the kids burst out of the cars bundled in their puffy jackets and squealing with excitement. Janet jumped right in, sledding down the hill with the kids, laughing as loud as they did, and tossing snowballs with perfect aim. By the end of the day, the little ones were sprawled across couches, sipping hot chocolate with rosy cheeks and heavy eyelids, while the adults played board games and shared stories late into the night. Life couldn't be better.

But then the headaches started. At first, Janet brushed them off as stress or fatigue, but gradually they grew stronger, sharper, harder to ignore. Finally, she agreed to see the doctor. That first visit didn't give us many answers, only more questions and a lingering sense of unease. Looking back, it marked the beginning of a journey neither of us could have imagined, a journey that would test every vow we had spoken on our wedding day.

I can still see her at the dinner table that night, smiling through the pain so the kids wouldn't notice, her strength on full display even as something inside her was breaking.

LIFTED Value: **Transform Through Hope** Hope is not about ignoring reality. It is about believing in a better future while addressing the harsh truths of the present.

Lifted Insight:

"For a moment, the world stopped, my mind going blank and racing all at once. It wasn't possible; not one, not two, but several doctors had told me this could never happen. Did I hear her right? Did she really just say we're having a baby?"

Leadership Reflection: When has something you thought impossible become possible, and how did that reshape your hope as a leader?

CHAPTER 11

The Empty Chair

The scent of antiseptic was the first thing to hit us, a sharp, cold sting that seemed to precede the chill penetrating our skin, when we walked into the doctor's office that day. Without looking too deeply, he said her headaches were most likely typical migraines, and he would prescribe some medication to manage the pain. He gave us a referral to a migraine clinic that could give her more support. His words comforted me, knowing we may have found the answer.

As we left the clinic, the sterile scent of the office fading behind us, we stepped into the parking lot. I felt the tension drain from my shoulders. The sun felt a little warmer, the air a little lighter. I caught myself smiling for the first time in days, the simple promise of 'normal' a balm to a wound I hadn't even realized was festering, was present. For a moment, I wanted to believe this was the end of it, but a quiet unease was still there.

The next day I went back to work, and Janet slipped into caring for the kids and the house. When I walked in that evening, the children barreled toward me shouting, "Daddy!" Their laughter filled the room as the smell of baked chicken and rosemary wrapped around us. For a moment, everything felt right. With my heart full, I asked how she was feeling.

"I'm OK, Stefan. The pain medication is helping." She said it lightly, almost too quickly, her calm masking something deeper. Janet never wanted to burden anyone, least of all me. I couldn't shake the feeling she was protecting me.

Janet soldiered on for months, cooking, folding laundry, and shuttling the kids to school as if nothing were wrong. On Sundays she came alive at church, singing hymns with eyes closed and her hand resting on Gaby's hair. At game nights she laughed with friends, though I sometimes caught her eyes clouding when she thought no one was looking. Beckie and Amber checked in often, slipping away for coffee while the kids were at school. I admired how she clung to normal life, but a quiet fear gnawed at me.

Six months later, we took a trip to La Jolla with some friends, a place I had loved as a child. I wanted our kids to have those same memories by the ocean. Janet joined in, running with the kids along the shoreline and laughing with Janet as they made sandwiches in the hotel room. For a while it felt like life was the way it should be. But no matter how she really felt, Janet would smile and insist she was fine. After a day or two she started slipping away, retreating to a dark room where the curtains were pulled shut. That was when I knew her pain was piercing.

I found her lying on the bed in a dark room with the curtains drawn tight. "Are you OK?" I asked.

"The light is bothering me," she whispered. For Janet to retreat like this, the pain had to be unbearable. "I just need to rest a while," she said.

"Do you want to go home?" I asked.

"No, no Stefan. I will be OK. Just give me a little time."

I nodded and stepped out, my chest heavy. She was pushing through for the kids, and I felt powerless to take the pain away.

She drifted in and out of the bedroom for the rest of the trip. One moment she was with us, smiling faintly as the kids played, and the

THE EMPTY CHAIR

next she was gone again behind the closed door. I tried to convince myself it was just exhaustion, but each time she disappeared my stomach tightened. By the time we packed up to leave, the skies outside were bright, and the sun streamed through the windows, warming her face as we drove home. With her eyes closed, she whispered, "Stefan, when we get home, I want to check my vision." The migraine medicine was no longer helping, and now she seemed certain the problem was her eyesight.

The optometrist listened carefully as we explained what had been happening. Janet described the dizziness, nausea, the sharp pain, and the tingling that ran across her face and down her arms. She told her about the night she thought she might be having a stroke, and how the emergency room had sent her home without a scan. Even with the migraine treatments, the headaches were only getting worse. When the doctor leaned in to examine her, I felt myself holding my breath. *Finally, we are going to get an answer,* I thought.

The doctor's expression changed in an instant. The easy smile was gone, replaced by a look of urgency that made my stomach drop. She reached for her prescription pad, her hand trembling as the pen scratched across the paper. When she handed it to Janet, her eyes locked on mine over the top of her glasses, sharp and unflinching. Scrawled across the slip were the words *MRI STAT.* My chest tightened. This was no longer about migraines. "Take this to the emergency room," she said.

We left the office stunned, as if the world itself was pressing down on my chest, the crushing force making it hard to breathe. Neither of us spoke on the drive. I kept my eyes on the road, but my mind was racing. If it was serious enough to write *MRI STAT,* what did that mean for Janet? For the kids? For us?

The waiting room air was thick with disinfectant and stale coffee. A low hum of coughs and sniffles filled the space. Janet and I sat close in a corner, watching the flicker of a muted television while a woman across from us tugged nervously at her mask.

153

I braced myself for hours of waiting, but within minutes they called Janet back and rushed her in for an MRI. My chest lifted with a flicker of hope. Maybe this was just routine. Maybe the urgency was about ruling things out, not uncovering something life-altering. When the nurse finished, she handed us discharge papers and said the doctor would call with results. Relief tugged at me, but it was thin and fragile. *Why would they send us home if this was something dangerous?*

That relief evaporated the moment we pulled into the driveway. The phone rang. Janet's doctor told us to return to the hospital immediately. She would meet us there. Then she hung up. Janet turned to me, her voice calm but searching. "Stefan, what do you think it could be?"

I swallowed hard, but I forced my voice to sound steady. "Let's see what they found and we'll work through it together."

Her doctor met us at the hospital, her calm but serious look sending a shiver through me. She drew scans and lit them on the wall. My eyes fixed on the ghostly shapes, not wanting to believe what I was seeing. She pointed to the lesions scattered across her brain. Twelve could be counted, though she warned there might be more hidden beneath the swelling. With every word, the pressure on my chest became more intense.

The swelling had already shifted her brain slightly from the midpoint. It was dangerous, she said. They needed to admit her immediately, start steroids, and bring the swelling down. She admitted they didn't know if it was tumors or something. Tests would continue.

In my denial, I argued with my worried self. I thought of my own benign tumor, *Maybe that's what she has. Maybe it's just a cyst that can be treated. Maybe it is not as bad as it looks.*

We began making calls to our friends, arranging care for the kids. Natalie and Jenny stepped in right away, since their children went to school with ours. They loved our kids as if they were their own, keeping them busy with play and comfort. Amber and Beckie coordinated meals through the church, and before we knew it, casseroles and prayers were flowing steadily into our home. Our children who were twelve, nine, seven, and four, sensed something was wrong. With shadows behind their smiles, they clung to the comfort of our friends.

In the days that followed, when Janet was resting, I would be found in the hospital chapel. The silence was heavy, broken only by the sound of footsteps outside. I bowed my head, buried my face in my hands, and cried out to God. *Please God, let this be something that can be healed. My life has already been so hard, but you have always been there. Be here now. Please do not take her away. Please, God, please.* In my desperation I even tried to bargain with Him. *Take more from me if you must. Give me the pain, but please let her live.*

The tears were steaming down my face. Sitting in the chapel, I felt the same crushing loneliness I remembered from childhood nights in my room, when I was terrified of living life alone. What if that was the moment it came true? What if I lost Janet, and our kids were left without her?

Then our pastor, Greg Rhodes entered. He didn't come with long speeches or explanations. He sat beside me, a steady hand on my shoulder, and prayed quietly over us. His presence did not take away the fear, but it calmed the storm inside me just enough to face what was ahead. I wiped my tears, took a deep breath, and returned to Janet's room.

As the swelling in Janet's brain began to ease, she felt some relief. For a moment I let myself believe my prayers might be working, that maybe God was answering. But even in that flicker of hope, the old fear clung tight. The thought of living life without her, of raising our kids alone was something I couldn't imagine. My heart swung back and forth between best case and worst case, as if I had no control over the thoughts invading my mind.

The whirlwind from the optometrist to the ER to the scan results left us dazed. Moving only on instinct, we finally returned home. The refrigerator quickly filled with meals, and friends surrounded us with comfort. For Janet, it was Amber and Beckie she leaned on most, the ones who prayed with her, sat beside her, and gave her strength when I could not. For our children, it was Natalie and Jenny. Since their kids went to school together, they knew how to steady ours with love that felt safe and familiar. Sophia, Amelia, Samuel, and little Gaby were hugged, distracted, and cared for as if they were their own.

Even with all that help, I noticed a new look in our children's eyes. Their smiles couldn't hide the worry that lingered beneath. Gaby clung to Janet's leg as if holding her there could keep her from slipping away. Watching it all, I felt torn in two, unable to console them. I was grateful for the love surrounding us, yet the fear gripped me.

Janet rested in bed for the next several days while friends moved in and out of the house like a gentle tide. They brought food, circled us in prayer, and filled the silence with kindness. Amber and Beckie became her closest companions that season. They were the ones she trusted enough to cry with, the ones who gave her strength when I could not. Their prayers, their laughter, even their quiet presence reminded Janet she was not facing this alone.

I was grateful for Natalie and Jenny. They picked the kids up from school, helped with homework, and made sure our kids' days stayed steady when everything else felt uncertain. They loved our children as if they were their own, giving Sophia, Amelia, Samuel, and little Gaby the security of being cared for without question.

Even with this circle of love, I had to hold it together for Janet and the kids, ignoring my own fear, as our life became a series of appointments and daily medications. The daunting list of medications included many that were taken to counter the effects of the others. Our normal life had slipped away, and I found myself longing for it with an ache that cut deep.

The side-effects of steroids took their toll. Janet lashed out at times and wept at others. Though I knew it was the medicine, it was hard to watch. When her moods swung, I would guide the kids out of the room, then return to sit with her until it passed. Sometimes she apologized.

Sometimes she sat in silence, too drained to speak. It became part of our rhythm. Pain, tears, laughter, prayer. Through it all, we pressed on. We were the Beans, and somehow we found a way forward. Ironically, during this time of struggle, my school was doing well. When I'd go to work it was difficult to compartmentalize it from my life, but I welcomed the distraction of the daily grind.

It was my fourth year as principal at Gateway Elementary and we were finally on track. My focus on developing a positive school culture improved as teachers and staff members embraced working together, With a common vision and mission, everyone felt they were valued and our teams finally started collaborating for a common goal. Our students started to thrive. Our campus was a happier place; kids were learning and as test scores soared. In between each success and happy feeling, a sense of doom crept in monopolizing any little bit of joy. *How could work be going well when the rest of my world was falling apart?*

Janet's next appointment was a full body scan that showed the rest of her body was clear of any problems except one swollen lymph node under her left arm. Having ruled out parasites, they finally had something they could biopsy. Our worst nightmare came true that day: Janet had cancer.

It was breast cancer that spread to her brain. Hearing the word itself was a physical blow, a punch to the gut that took my breath away. My vision blurred and my head spun. I couldn't feel my body. I looked at Janet, searching her face for a hint of her usual strength, but even she seemed to have been knocked off her axis. My tears could not release the severe pain in the pit of my stomach as I sat in shock. *How were we going to get through this? Oh my God, the kids. How am I going to take care of everybody? How am I going to take care of her?*

Reinforced by our faith, we gathered the kids and told them the truth in words they could understand. Mom was sick. The doctors would try to help her with treatments, and we would pray for healing. We told them to give their worries to God, that *He* had a plan even if we could not see it. Their puzzled faces broke my heart. They were scared, and so was I, but there was no way around it. We had to walk into the unknown together, hand in hand, trusting that God would be by our side.

The doctors laid out the plan: Two kinds of chemotherapy to stop the cancer from spreading every three weeks indefinitely, and whole brain radiation for five days to target the tumors. Driving to Los Angeles for treatments became our new routine. Janet faced it all with a quiet fierceness I had never seen before. She never complained, never flinched. Even strapped to machines, she spoke with nurses and doctors about faith, offering them encouragement when she was the one in need. Her strength humbled me.

The treatments were working. Her tumors were shrinking, which reduced the swelling in her brain, but the mood swings from the steroids continued. One day her lashing out came in handy when a hospital worker yelled at a homeless woman who made a mess in the bathroom. Janet raised her voice, "You don't treat people like that. She was made in God's image, too!" But she did not stop there. She stood, entered the bathroom and cleaned it herself.

Over time, the swelling in her brain reduced as the chemo began shrinking the tumors, and she started to feel better. When Janet felt some relief, a tiny, desperate flicker of hope ignited inside me. I clung to it. Maybe, just maybe, my prayers were being answered. My thoughts still flipped from best case to worst, as if my mind was on autopilot, but for the moment the worst seemed a little further away.

Janet met that moment with courage. She shaved her head, laced up her shoes, and walked a half marathon with Kalima from church. The sight of her moving with such determination, bare scalp shining in the sun, was unforgettable. For a while she felt unstoppable, and she was. It gave us a moment of hope to hold on to, a fleeting signal of improvement that gave us the strength to keep fighting.

As treatments continued, Janet's friends surrounded her in ways that only true friends could. Amber brought her laughter and prayer, reminding her that joy was still possible even in the hardest moments. She often took Janet to appointments when I was at work, her steady presence lifting some of the weight from both of us. Beckie became her late-night companion, the one who answered the phone at two in the morning when Janet could not sleep. They prayed together, talked through her fears, and sometimes stayed on the line until the sun came up.

One night I woke and Janet was gone. Panic consumed me as I called Amber, who jumped into her car to help me look. She found Janet walking toward church at four in the morning, determined to be in the one place she felt closest to God. On other nights when she couldn't sleep, I would wake up to find her planting flowers in the terrace garden or scrubbing the stove before dawn. Her body was worn down, yet her spirit kept searching for peace.

Needing to know, at our next visit we pressed the oncologist about time. His answer was quiet but firm. Most patients with metastatic breast cancer to the brain lived about six months. These words were beyond devastating. At that moment, knowing became worse than not knowing.

On the drive home, the heaviness of silence lingered until Janet finally spoke. She looked out the window, after much thought, and then said, "Stefan, God promised me extended days." I did not know what to say. But I could see in her eyes that she meant it, and somehow I chose to believe her.

God gave us six more years. For five of those years, Janet was relatively healthy, and our kids had the gift of a mom who showed up in all the normal ways, helping with homework, cooking dinners, cheering at baseball games, and sitting in the front row with a beanie on her head. But woven through those years were two more rounds of radiation, a brain surgery, a broken hip due to imbalance, a half a dozen stays in rehab, and lengthy hospital visits.

There were stretches when the kids would not see their mom for days, and we leaned heavily on the care of our community. Jenny loved Gaby as if she were her own daughter, never once complaining as she gave her rides and cared for her while I was at the hospital. Natalie kept the older kids grounded, making sure their routines stayed steady. Our school, work, and church communities all lifting us through this terrible season of life through prayers, meals, rides and comfort. Her sisters, Lucy and Tricia, came down from Hanford often, helping Janet through long recoveries after surgeries and filling our home with support we desperately needed.

The battle changed our marriage completely, as I tried to divide myself into a million pieces. Between being present for the kids, caring for Janet in the hospital, and progressing in my leadership role, I was stretched thin. All this division often left her feeling lonely. We both longed for the simplicity of what we once had together, yet the demands of cancer always seemed to come first. I carried hope, but alongside it an unshakable sense of doom and anxiety was always there. As the last two years unfolded, I saw her health begin to deteriorate. Each decline chipped away at my fragile belief that this fight would last.

Through it all, we kept our family traditions alive. We went on our annual vacations, set up tents on camping trips, and made memories that could never be stolen by cancer. Those years were not easy, but they were filled with life, and they were ours.

But beneath the surface of family dinners and school plays, our reality was a constant battle. The medications piled up on the kitchen counter, each one a tie to this relentless disease. We became experts at reading the subtle shifts in Janet's mood and energy, our lives a carefully choreographed dance around her good days and bad. The peace we felt was always hard-won, a brief stillness in the long, dark corridor we were walking.

Photo of the Bean family.
Photo from Stefan Bean's personal photo library.

Janet would defy all odds with her determination and faith, following her conversation with God, to live six more years to see our babies grow up: Sophia to eighteen, Amelia fifteen, Samuel thirteen, and Gaby ten. Our children had their mom during the years they needed her most.

Janet's decline accelerated rapidly in her final year. We prayed for a miracle with all our might and clung to every speck of hope, but she finally required twenty-four-hour respite care from home. She became noncommunicative and bedridden. I could not lift her, turn her, or help her in and out of bed, so God led others to stand in the gap. Janet's niece Brittany, her brother Tony, and our oldest daughter Sophia cared for her physical needs, and Sally supported us by keeping the house together. Amelia, Samuel, and Gabriella would also help in their own ways. Their presence was a lifeline.

Yet their help also stirred something deep inside me. I remembered Janet's prophetic words from long ago: "I don't think I can marry you because when I am old and sick, you will not be able to care for me." At the time I brushed it aside, convinced it would never happen. But now those words wrapped around me like a chain. She knew and she was right. I could not care for her the way I wanted, and the truth crushed me.

Even so, I knew I could not let that truth destroy me. The guilt pressed heavy, but I held fast to the belief that God brought Brittany, Tony, Sally, and my children to do what I couldn't. Their presence was not my failure. It was the way it was supposed to be, even if it was hard for me to see it that way, we were blessed.

Before she lost her ability to speak fully, she looked at me, took my hand in hers, and whispered her last intelligible words: "Babe...I love you...promise to take care of the kids." Her voice was weak but steady, carrying the same love and trust she had given me from the start. At that moment I understood her words as a plea for our children. Of course I would care for them with everything in me.

Looking back now, I believe Janet's words carried something more. She was asking me to care not only for Sophia, Amelia, Samuel, and Gaby, but also for every child entrusted to me in my role as a leader. It was her way of reminding me that love and responsibility extend beyond our home and into the lives of the children I would continue to serve.

Months passed after Janet lost her ability to speak, move, and respond. Even then she fought to stay with us. Though she could not tell us, we knew she was still aware, still hearing our voices, still present in the room. At times she would raise her hand listening to a worship song, or grasp ours with surprising strength when she wanted to tell us something. Other times she met our eyes and held them, a quiet signal that she was still with us. We talked to her, prayed with her, and stayed close, believing she understood every word. Her strength showed itself in her sheer will to remain with us, even when her body had given way.

Somehow, every close friend came to visit the night Janet went to heaven. The house felt full, almost as if God had arranged for a gathering to carry us through what was about to happen. The kids were in the family room, surrounded by laughter and games, held close by people who loved them. For a few brief hours, life in that room felt safe and almost ordinary.

In Janet's room, the air was quieter, heavier. Amber, Beckie, and I prayed by her side, our voices soft and steady as her breathing slowed. My mind flooded with memories of our life together, each one flashing by like a reel I could not stop. With one last exhale, she gave her final breath as I watched, and her spirit slipped gently into God's hands. When it was only her and me, I leaned in and gave her one final kiss goodbye.

Not long after, we called everyone in, and together we surrounded Janet, hand in hand, lifting prayers over her. It felt like a sacred circle, a reminder that the same community who had walked with us from the very beginning of this cancer journey was with us at the end. Janet's illness was heavy, but I had to inspire hope for my family even while grieving. I needed my children to see that the community would empower us through the valleys of our lives.

Between those two kisses stretched a lifetime of love. She went where I could not follow, but I hold to the hope that I will see her again. Until that day, I see her in our children. In their kindness, their determination, their faith, I catch glimpses of Janet, her legacy written into their lives. Surrounded by silence and prayer, I felt her love lifting me, a strength that would carry me forward even as life would never be the same.

> Between those two kisses stretched a lifetime of love.

Photo of Janet Bean Memorial,
Photo from the personal photo library of Stefan Bean, November 27, 2020.

Rest in Peace, Beautiful Janet.

LIFTED Value: **Empower Others** Empowering others is about committing to walk alongside people, offering support and trust, rather than leading from afar. True empowerment happens in proximity, not separation.

Lifted Insight:

"Janet's illness was heavy, but I had to inspire hope for my family even while grieving. I needed my children to see that the community would empower us through the valleys of our lives."

Leadership Reflection: What role does trust play in empowering others when life feels heavy?

CHAPTER 12

~

Her Last Request,
My Lifelong Mission

Janet's last words, "Take care of the kids" echoed in my mind as I walked into my office the first day back to work after losing Janet. My mind lit up with an "aha moment" I wasn't expecting. Janet wasn't just talking about taking care of *our* kids, she was talking about taking care of *every* child under my umbrella of leadership. Her final request to me expanded my mission as an educational leader, a call to listen and to develop every child. This epiphany illuminated my responsibility as superintendent in Los Angeles, and propelled it to a more meaningful level; suddenly everything made sense.

In that instant, the roles of a single father and superintendent merged into one mission. It was as if all the moments of being lifted in my life, from the orphanage in Saigon, to the dinner table lessons with my diverse siblings, to the friends who carried me up staircases, suddenly came into focus. Her parting words were not just about survival; they were a commission for a greater purpose.

On the long drive back that day, I replayed the words of my children at Janet's service. Amelia stood with quiet strength and read her mother's favorite Bible verse: *"Do not be anxious about anything, but in every situation, by prayer and petition, with thanksgiving, present your requests to God.*" Sophia spoke of her mother's reminder that "We might be the only Bible anyone ever sees," weaving her into the very fabric of her own identity. And sweet Gabriella recalled the small rituals

> Her parting words were not just about survival; they were a commission for a greater purpose.

of dark chocolate with her mom, whispering, "You're the best mom ever." In their words I heard not only grief, but also wisdom beyond their years. They were reminding me, even in their loss, that we still had one another, and that Janet's spirit would remain in us. We would never move on but together we would move forward.

To hold onto that hope, we leaned on counseling and the community around us. It reminded me of something I had discovered long before, the Stockdale Paradox. Admiral Stockdale taught that true resilience comes from facing brutal facts while never losing faith in the end of the story. My children were now living that paradox. They faced the harsh truth of life without their mom, yet they carried forward her strength and faith as a light for their future. I knew then that my leadership would need to follow the same pattern, honest about reality but anchored in hope.

Our Bethany Church friends surrounded us with steady support in those first months, checking in, bringing meals, and reminding us we were not alone. That same spirit spread into our neighborhood, where friends became like family. Natalie walked the kids to school and talked with Janet about life. Jenny, balancing work and her own children, still opened her home to Gabriella after school. And Sally, once Janet's caregiver, kept coming weekly to help in the house. Together, these women became mother figures for my children, each carrying a piece of Janet's love forward.

Those experiences reminded me of the first leadership value: *listen and learn*. True leadership does not begin with a plan or a directive, it begins with paying attention. Just as I listened at our dinner table growing up, where every sibling had a voice, I now listened to my children and to the families in our community. I have always said in my leadership positions that when we include the people who are most affected by decisions in the decision-making process, that is truly listening to lead. Their needs, their fears, their small acts of resilience shaped the way I led. I learned that leadership is not about carrying the load alone, but about creating space for others to carry pieces of it with you.

With the love and support of family, church and neighborhood friends, we discovered we could do more than survive. We could move forward knowing that Janet was still with us, not left behind, but carried in the choices we made and in the way we lived. And it was in that realization that the second leadership value came alive: *inspire potential*. Janet had always seen strengths in people that they did not see in themselves. Now it was my turn to help my children, our staff, and our students recognize the gifts they carried within them. In my professional life, I found the same to be true with my teammates. When I recognized and cultivated their potential, I watched motivation grow, energy rise, and a deeper sense of ownership take root.

Sophia went on to USC to major in biological sciences, and I teared up when she told me she was working at the Lyon Center, the place where her mother and I first met. She carried forward her mother's conviction, choosing to dedicate her life caring for all of God's creation.

Amelia, strong and determined like her mother, faced the milestones of high school without Janet by her side. I stood with her for prom pictures, cheered her at graduation, and watched her rise with grit. Now at Berkeley, pursuing legal studies with plans for law school, Amelia shows me that inspiring potential often means simply standing with someone as they discover their path.

Samuel, a kind and joyous soul who drew people in like Janet did, flourished in high school with a wide circle of friends. His intellect came easily, but his compassion was the greater strength. With plans to attend college and become a chemist, he reminds me that potential is not always about pushing harder, but about recognizing the quiet gifts that can bless others for a lifetime.

Gabriella, the youngest, carried the sweetness and warmth of her mother into every space. Middle school was hard without Janet, but Jenny, her second mom, helped guide her through those years. Watching Gabriella grow reminded me that even the youngest voices carry deep potential, and they thrive when surrounded by love, patience, and encouragement.

In each of my children I saw the same truth I carried into leadership. Potential is not something we force, it is something we notice, nurture, and believe in long before it becomes visible. Whether with my children, my students, or my staff, I learned that when people know you believe in them, they will begin to believe in themselves. That realization carried me into the next lesson of leadership: the importance of *fostering authenticity*.

Amidst the cloudiness of my grief, my mission in life became clear, and Janet was the reason for that clarity. I realized that leadership for me could never be about appearances or titles. It had to be about living honestly, scars and all, and allowing others to see that grief and strength can live side by side. I could not move on from Janet, but I could carry her forward by leading in a way that was real.

At work, this meant I no longer felt the pressure to act as if everything was fine. I shared openly with colleagues and parents about the challenges of raising four children alone, and in turn they trusted me with their own struggles. I discovered that authenticity builds a kind of credibility that no credentials ever could. People do not need perfect leaders; they need honest ones.

Looking back, I realized I had learned this lesson long before. As a boy, sitting at the dinner table with my siblings, or later when Mr. Geisinger asked me to give oral presentations instead of written ones, I was being invited to show up as my true self. Those experiences taught me that *fostering authenticity* is the foundation of trust. Now, as superintendent and as a single father, I leaned on that truth every day.

When COVID arrived in 2020, everything changed overnight. Schools closed, families were thrown into crisis, and leaders everywhere scrambled to find answers none of us had. A single mother called me one day in tears, torn between keeping her job and leaving her children home alone without internet or food. Her desperation reminded me that this was not about systems or policies. It was about people.

At that moment, I understood the importance of *fostering authenticity*. I could not pretend to have quick solutions. What I could do was lead with honesty about the challenges and empathize with the pain families were carrying. I began every morning checking in with principals, not just about student learning, but also about how they were holding up as parents themselves. I shared openly about my own struggles as a single father, trying to juggle work and home while still grieving Janet. My willingness to be vulnerable created a space where others could be real about their exhaustion and fears.

That authenticity deepened trust across the district. Parents trusted us because we acknowledged the challenges. Teachers trusted us because we listened instead of pretending to have all the answers. Students trusted us because they saw adults show up with honesty and compassion. Fostering authenticity did not weaken leadership; it strengthened it. It reminded everyone that leadership is not about presenting a polished image, it is about creating a safe space for people to bring their whole selves—fears, scars, and all—and to know they will be supported.

When in-person school resumed after the pandemic, the challenges did not vanish. Some students were terrified to return, others had disengaged entirely, and families were still trying to regain their footing. Attendance boards showed not only behavior concerns but deeper issues of trauma, loss, and fear. It was tempting to see only the problems, but I knew that leadership meant helping people see beyond what was broken.

This was where the value of *transforming through hope* came alive. Hope was not about ignoring reality. It was about believing in a better future while addressing the harsh truths of the present. I thought back to my own life, the surgeries that left me in a full body cast, the moments in Saigon when survival felt impossible, the years of rejection when I longed for love. Every time, I had to cling to hope even when the facts told me otherwise. That same paradox was now what our students and families needed.

I reminded staff that consequences alone would not solve the struggles we were seeing. We needed to peel back the layers of pain and meet students with compassion. We needed to *model* hope, not just talk about it. I shared my own journey with them, not to draw attention to myself, but to show that despair does not have the final word. If I could survive those early years and find purpose, then our students could discover their own strength too.

Transforming through hope became our compass. We adjusted plans again and again, supported mental health needs, and created spaces where students could believe in a future worth striving for. Hope did not erase the struggles, but it gave us the energy to keep moving forward together.

Yet even as our schools found their footing, I struggled with my own. How could I create a sustainable rhythm for myself as a single father while still carrying the daily weight of grief? The two-hour drive to and from work kept me away from my children at the very time they needed me most. I knew I had to change. Leadership for me could no longer be defined by distance or position. It had to start closer to home, where my presence mattered most.

The race for County Superintendent of Schools in Orange County became a defining moment in that journey. I knew the larger the platform, the more leaders I could empower, which meant the more students I could serve, nearly half a million. Campaigning was exhausting, filled with endless events and late nights, and in the end I did not win. But what I gained was clarity. Strength is not measured by a title. Strength is found in the ability to *empower others*, whether in a county of millions or in your own home.

Although I lost, I accepted a role as executive director of a charter organization in Irvine that was struggling to survive. Many had already written it off, but I saw the possibility. By empowering the team with trust, responsibility, and conviction, we began to turn things around. In just two years we increased enrollment by three hundred percent and the school was recognized with the California Distinguished School award. Even when all seemed lost, strength was found in sharing ownership and showing people that they already carried what was needed. That experience reminded me that empowerment always begins with presence. My children needed to see that their father was not only providing, but also available. My staff needed to know that I trusted them with real responsibility. And my community needed to feel that I was committed to walking alongside them, not leading from afar.

That same lesson prepared me for what came next. Hearing that I had been appointed the twelfth County Superintendent of Schools for Orange County was an honor I never imagined possible. I could feel Janet smiling as one-by-one Mari, Ken, Tim, Lisa and Jorge unanimously voted yes for me to be the next leader. I was humbled to know I was being entrusted with a position that would influence and impact so many. It was also deeply meaningful to know that I was the first Asian American Pacific Islander leader to hold this role since 1889, a reminder that representation matters for the students and families we serve.

In my first hundred days, I listened and learned, meeting with more than thirty district leaders over breakfasts and lunches, including representatives from twenty-eight school districts, community colleges, and Regional Occupational Programs. Many expressed gratitude simply for being heard. In each conversation, I felt Mr. Geisinger with me, the teacher who once gave me a voice, now present as I gave a voice to others. When the day came for me to be sworn in, he traveled from San Diego to administer the oath. Only twelve people had held this office since 1889, and in that moment I felt the weight of history, the presence of Janet, and the grace of a story come full circle. After the oath, I leaned toward him and whispered, "Thank you, Mr. G, for empowering me for this moment."

Within the scope of my duties, I was now in charge of the most vulnerable students; incarcerated youth, homeless youth, and students with mild to severe disabilities. Standing before these students, I realized my own journey had brought me to this specific place. I was a man who had been lifted, and now I was in a position to be a lifeline for the most vulnerable. I was exactly where I was meant to be, *developing others* by inspiring potential in students who needed it most.

The highlight of my career was sitting with incarcerated youth each month, not as an authority figure but as a mentor. We would talk about life and play cribbage, just as my grandfather once did with me. In those moments, I was not only teaching them a game but showing them that they were worth someone's time, that their voices and futures still mattered. *Developing others* meant helping them imagine a different ending to their story.

I handed diplomas to students whose parents never thought they would graduate, but who discovered strength when someone believed in them. I stood at ceremonies for youth with severe disabilities and reminded them that their lives carried unique gifts the world was waiting to receive. My mother had instilled that same truth in me when she pushed me to do chores, climb stairs, and face challenges head-on. Now, I passed it on to them: Your limitations do not define you, your determination does.

Developing others became the thread running through every part of my leadership. It was in coaching principals, building trust with district leaders, and mentoring young people who doubted their worth. It

> Your limitations do not define you, your determination does.

was never about my success alone but about ensuring that others had the opportunity to grow, thrive, and lead.

I am not here because I am extraordinary. I am here because ordinary people did extraordinary things for me. They developed me, empowered me, believed in me. And my charge now is simple: do the same for others. Be someone's lift. Janet showed me what that looked like every day of her life, in the way she loved our children, supported her friends, and encouraged me to lead with both courage and compassion. Her influence lives on not only in our family but in every student, teacher, and leader I have the privilege to serve.

Leadership is not a ladder to climb, but a hand to reach out. It begins with *listening and learning,* creating space for every voice to be heard. It is *inspiring potential,* seeing strengths in others they cannot yet see in themselves. It is *fostering authenticity,* leading with honesty and vulnerability so others feel safe to be real. It is *transforming through hope,* holding on when circumstances feel overwhelming and showing that despair never has the final word. It is *empowering through strength,* entrusting people with meaningful responsibility and cheering them on as they grow. And it is *developing others,* investing in their future so the mission outlives you. Leadership is the act of love, the steady hand that lifts others, and ultimately the legacy we leave behind.

And in all this, I still see Janet's handprints. She taught me what authentic love looks like, what courage sounds like, and what it means to lift others even in the hardest seasons. Her spirit remains the quiet strength behind every part of this framework, and her influence continues to guide the way I lead today.

This is what it means to be *lifted to lead.*

Photo of Stefan, Sophia, Amelia, Samuel, and Gabriella.
Photo from Stefan Bean's personal photo album.

LIFTED Value: **Develop Others** Developing others means fostering long-term growth and potential, ensuring the mission continues beyond the leader.

Lifted Insight:

"Janet wasn't just talking about taking care of our kids, she was talking about taking care of every child under my umbrella of leadership. Her final request to me expanded my mission as an educational leader, a call to listen and to develop every child. This epiphany illuminated my responsibility as superintendent in Los Angeles, and propelled it to a more meaningful level; suddenly everything made sense. "

Leadership Reflection: How do you ensure the people you lead are prepared to continue the mission after you?

The Final Lift

As I come to the end of this story, I want to pause and just say thanks. Thank you for walking with me through the memories, the struggles, the heartbreak, and the triumphs that have shaped my life. Thank you for holding these stories close enough to see not only where I came from, but also what I hope we all might carry forward together.

I did not make it here alone. My journey has been one of being lifted, time and time again, by people who saw something in me even when I could not see it in myself. From the streets of Saigon to the superintendent's chair, every step of the way has been marked by others reaching out, believing in me, and giving me the strength to keep going. I will always be grateful to Greg and Judy Bean, who first lifted me from being an abandoned child to being a son. Their decision to open their hearts and home to many of us changed the entire trajectory of our lives. And I will never forget Mr. Geisinger, my sixth-grade teacher, who believed in my voice before I did and taught me that words could lift others, a lesson that has shaped my life as a leader.

To my children, Sophia, Amelia, Gabriella, and Samuel, you are the reason I keep pushing forward. You are my greatest joy and my greatest responsibility. You are proof that love rewrites even the most complex stories. When the doctors told us that children would never be possible, I could not have imagined that God would bless me with four of the most beautiful lives I have ever known. Each of you carries a piece of your mother, and together you carry her whole spirit.

Sophia, you are steady, compassionate, and wise beyond your years. You remind me so much of your mother in the way you care for others without asking for anything in return. Amelia, your drive and curiosity inspire me. You pursue knowledge and experience with a boldness that gives me hope for the world you are shaping. Gabriella, your laughter fills our home with light. You carry resilience inside of you that I know will serve you in ways you do not yet see. And Samuel, my son, you remind me daily of the joy of being alive. Your presence has lifted me in ways I cannot put into words.

Children, I want you to know this: the legacy I leave is not measured in titles or accomplishments. It is measured in you. If I have lifted others, it is because I was first lifted by your mother and by each of you. I hope that when you face trials of your own, you will remember the story we carry and know that you are never alone. You come from love. You come from strength. You come from faith.

To Janet, you may have given me our first kiss, but I was honored to give you our last. My love for you has never faded. You gave me the gift of a lifetime. You walked beside me with faith and courage. You pushed me when I doubted myself, and you steadied me when the storms came. I will never forget the day you jumped into the river to save my wheelchair. At that moment, I realized you weren't just saving metal and wheels, you were saving me. That was who you were: fearless, selfless, determined to make sure I could keep moving forward. You saw the man I could become long before I ever did. You gave me laughter, children, and the kind of love that people spend their whole lives searching for. And in your final moments, when you asked me to take care of the children, you raised me once again. That request became my anchor. It became the mission that has guided every decision I have made since.

The chair at the table may be empty, but your place in my heart is not. It is full, and it always will be. I still talk to you in quiet moments. I still hear your voice in the laughter of our kids. I still feel your hand in mine when the challenges of leadership weigh heavily on me. You live on in all that we built together, and in all that I will carry forward in your name.

And to you, the reader, I hope my story has been more than just a memoir. My deepest prayer is that you see yourself in these pages, that you recognize the ways you have been lifted in your own life, and that you find the courage to lift others. I am not here because I am extraordinary. I am here because of ordinary people who did extraordinary things for me. A mother and father who adopted me when I had no home. Teachers who believed I could lead. Friends who carried me when I could not climb the stairs. A wife who loved me unconditionally and taught me what devotion truly means. Children who gave me strength to live with purpose.

> I am here because of ordinary people who did extraordinary things for me.

The truth is simple. Love lifts. Leadership is not about control or power or titles. It is about lifting others. It is about hearing voices that are often ignored. It is about inspiring people to see the potential within themselves. It is about fostering authenticity enough that others feel free to be themselves. It is about transforming through hope when life feels impossible. It is about empowering others to step forward with courage. And it is about developing the next generation so that the story continues long after we are gone.

If my story has taught me anything, it is that leadership is not a position, it is a gift. A gift given to us by a teacher, parent, mentor, friend. It is a gift you pass on to others. Each of us has the power to lift. We can each believe someone's promise. Each of us can empower others to lead.

Throughout this book, I have shared stories of how my life was shaped by the lifts of others: family, teachers, friends, mentors, colleagues, and my wife Janet. From those experiences, and from my years in leadership, a pattern emerged. Leadership at its best is not about control or titles. It is about lifting others.

The **LIFTED Framework** captures those lessons. It is both a reflection of my story and a guide for anyone who seeks to lead with empathy, courage, and purpose.

Listen and Learn

Leadership begins with listening. A leader creates trust when they sit across from principals, teachers, or students and ask questions before offering solutions. Listening honors voices that might otherwise go unheard and lays the foundation for trust.

Inspire Potential

Leaders inspire when they call out gifts others do not yet see. This might mean inviting a quiet team member to lead a project or giving a student the chance to shine in an unexpected way. Inspiration awakens people to strengths they may have overlooked in themselves.

Foster Authenticity

Authentic leaders model vulnerability. A CEO who admits, "This year stretched me more than I expected, and I learned from you," builds far more trust than one who pretends to have all the answers. Authenticity creates belonging and allows others to be fully themselves.

Transform through Hope

Hope fuels resilience. In times of crisis, whether a pandemic, a natural disaster, or a budget cut, leaders who speak honestly about challenges while holding a vision for what can still be achieved help their teams endure. Hope keeps despair from having the final word.

Empower through Strength

Empowerment comes when leaders entrust others with meaning-ful responsibility. Delegating is not just about getting things done, it is about showing people you believe in their capacity. When leaders empower, they multiply strength in the organization.

Develop Others

True leadership is measured not by what happens during your tenure, but by the leaders you raise for the future. Mentorship, coaching, and intentional investment in people ensure that the mission will continue long after you are gone.

The LIFTED framework is not meant to be a checklist. It is an invitation to see leadership as an act of lifting. Each value is simple, but when practiced consistently, it transforms individuals, teams, organizations, and communities.

My life was not what I expected, but it has been so much more than I prayed for. From the war-torn streets of Saigon, abandoned and nameless, to a seat at the table as superintendent of schools, I have lived a life that I never could have imagined. It was not an easy life, but it was a lifted life—a life lifted by love, by grace, and by people who chose to believe in it.

And so, I leave you with this:

May you **listen** and **learn**, as I was taught at the Bean family dinner table, where every child had a voice and every story mattered.

May you **inspire potential**, the way Mr. G inspired me when he pulled me aside and said, "You have a gift," changing the trajectory of my life.

May you **foster authenticity**, as Janet did when she loved me, scars and all, creating a place where I could be fully myself.

May you **transform through hope**, as my children did when their laughter carried me through the darkest nights of grief.

May you **empower through strength**, like Janet did the day she leapt into the river to save my wheelchair, reminding me that love takes action.

And may you **develop others**, as I strive to do now with my children and the students of Orange County, knowing the mission must outlive me.

This is the heart of the **LIFTED** framework.

This is my thank you. This is my promise to Sophia, Amelia, Gabriella, and Samuel. And this is my undying love for Janet. And above all, I am grateful to God, who lifted me into a story far greater than I could have written on my own.

Acknowledgements

From Stefan: First and foremost, I give thanks to Jesus, my Lord and Savior, who has carried me through every season of my life. His grace, strength, and faithfulness have been my foundation, and this book would not exist without His hand guiding each step.

To my wife Janet, you are the love of my life, the one who saw past my scars and loved me completely. I will never forget when you first told me you loved me, breaking through years of rejection and showing me what it meant to be truly chosen. Thank you for standing beside me and filling my life with grace and a love that will live in me forever.

To my children Sophia, Amelia, Samuel, and Gaby, who are my pride and joy, you inspire me to be a better man, father, and leader. Your laughter, courage, and curiosity give meaning to all that I do.

To my co-author and friend Kathy, thank you for your wisdom, patience, and gift of words. You helped bring clarity and depth to this project, shaping my story into something far greater than I could have written alone.

To the mentors who changed the trajectory of my life, beginning with Mr. Geisinger, who saw potential in me and gave me the gift of finding my voice, Pastors Greg Rhodes, David Rimoldi, and Ron Ottenad, who deepened my faith and taught me how to lead with compassion and conviction, and Bill Sanderson, Katherine Ford, and Roberta Benjamin, whose leadership, encouragement, and steady guidance have continued to shape me as a leader.

To my mom and dad, Greg and Judy Bean, who gave me not only a home but unconditional love that has shaped me forever. To my closest brother, Martin, thank you for always being by my side with loyalty, laughter, and love that have carried me through so many seasons of life.

To my second parents, Mark and Jan, and Maria and Tony, thank you for welcoming me into your lives with love, encouragement, and care that felt like family.

To Janet's family, Lucy, Tricia, Tony, Marcel, and to her niece Brittany, thank you for the love and care you surrounded her with, and for walking so closely with her through both joy and hardship.

To friends who have been like family, Mark and Heidi, Jason and Sandy, Eric and Sandy, Amber and Mike, Becky and Sean, Matt and Kim, Natalie, and Jenny, thank you for your encouragement, friendship, and the many ways you have stood with our family through life's ups and downs.

From Kathy: Thank you, Jesus, for your constant presence and countless blessings, especially for bringing Stefan Bean into my life. It has been an incredible honor and responsibility to co-write his journey from tragedy to triumph, celebrating his family and inspiring leaders to lead with heart.

I am deeply grateful to support Stefan and his family, contributing to his enduring legacy. Thank you, my friend, for your authenticity, vulnerability, grace, and brilliant inspiration as both a leader and a writer. It's clear why so many have uplifted Stefan, as he, in turn, uplifts others.

A heartfelt thank you to Stefan's friends and team for their support in writing this book. To our publisher, Jimmy Casas and team, thank you for believing in us and the impact *Lifted to Lead* will have on leaders everywhere, and for your significant contributions to leadership with *Culturize* and beyond. To Lainie Rowell, author of *Evolving With Gratitude*, thanks for your support and introduction.

To John Reynoso, my friend and mentor, you nurtured me to become a leader. To my students and staff of the past twenty-five years, you have inspired and challenged me to be better. You are the driving force behind *Lifted to Lead* and the *Lifted Leadership Framework*, which aims to empower leaders to serve you more effectively.

Finally, to my sons, Anthony and Jake, and my grandsons, Dylan, Dustin, and Dominick, you are the very reason for my existence. And to all my family and friends, thank you for your unwavering support and for continually uplifting me as we navigate life together.

References

World Health Organization, (2025). History of the Polio Vaccine, *A Crippling and Life-Threatening Disease.* https://www.who.int/news-room/spotlight/history-of-vaccination/history-of-polio-vaccination

Bruno, R.L., Frick, N.M. (1987). Stress and "Type A" behavior as precipitants of Post-Polio Sequelae. In LS Halstead and DO Wiechers (Eds.): Research and Clinical Aspects of the Late Effects of Poliomyelitis. White Plains: March of Dimes Research Foundation. (pp. 145-155).

Ford, Gerald R. (1975). *A Time to Heal: The Autobiography of Gerald R. Ford).* p. 252 Fordlibrarymuseum.org

Nesson, Ron. (1975). *It sure looks different from the inside.* p. 99. Fordlibrarymuseum.org,

Rosenwald, Michael S. (2021) Operation Babylift Echoed in Kabul's Chaos. pp. 1-2. thewashingtonpost.com

Griffes, S. (2025) *Operation Baby Lift: 50 Years On.* Holt International, Child Sponsorship and International Adoption Stories holtinternational.org

Weidenfeld, S. (1975). First Lady's Lady: With the Fords at the White House. Fordlibrarymuseum.org

Sexton, R. (1975). Article, Tiny Vietnamese Orphan Arrives In San Diego. San Diego, The Tribune. p. 1.

Collins, J. C. 1. (2001). Good to great: why some companies make the leap... and others don't. HarperBusiness. pp. 83-87.

Staff writer, (2025). Power of Hope: Teaching and Developing Hopeful Thinking in Students. Inspired Engagement. Inspired-engagement.com.

About the Authors

D r. Stefan Bean has dedicated the past twenty-eight years to serving Southern California communities and students as a teacher, principal, and school administrator. In June 2024, the Orange County Board of Education unanimously appointed him as Orange County's 12th superintendent of schools, a position that dates back to 1889.

From July 2022 through June 2024, Dr. Bean served as the executive director of the Irvine International Academy. Prior to this, he worked for Aspire Public Schools in Los Angeles for nearly twelve years, progressing through roles as lead principal, associate superintendent and superintendent. In the latter role, he oversaw eleven schools serving students from transitional kindergarten through grade 12.

His educational qualifications include a bachelor's degree from the University of Southern California, a master's degree in educational leadership from Loyola Marymount University and a doctorate in educational administration from California State University, Fullerton.

Dr. Bean's personal experiences as an English language learner and a student with a disability have deeply influenced his educational philosophy. He has expressed a particular passion for supporting English learners and marginalized students.

During his college years, Dr. Bean met Janet Soares, whom he married in 2000. They raised four children and were deeply involved in work and ministry. Dr. Bean credits Janet, who tragically passed away in 2020 after a battle with cancer, as a significant source of support throughout his life and career. Connect with Stefan: linkedin.com/in/drstefanbean or drbeanoc@proton.me or go to his website at www.liftedtolead.com

D r. Kathy Nash has dedicated twenty-five distinguished years to supporting students in her career in education. Her experience spans various roles, including elementary teacher

supporting special education, English learners, and gifted and talented students. As an elementary and middle school principal, she served in Title 1 schools, driven by a passion to empower leaders to serve marginalized youth.

Her commitment to fostering potential continued as a Title 1 coordinator for English learners and as a teacher on special assignment, where she inspired and empowered her staff. Her exceptional contributions were recognized with the titles of Teacher of the Year in Corona Norco Unified and ACSA Principal of the Year in Chino Unified.

Academically, Dr. Nash holds a Multiple Subject Teaching Credential, CLAD Certificate, Administrative Services Credential, a Master's Degree in Curriculum and Instruction, and a Doctorate Degree in Organizational Leadership. With her doctorate, she served as an adjunct professor, serving on a dissertation committee, and as a course developer for Brandman University (Umass Global) in extended education.

Beyond her administrative and teaching roles, Dr. Nash has significantly influenced educational policy. As a State Legislative committee member for ACSA on human resources and curriculum and instruction, she advocated for practical educational laws. She continues to make an impact through her published educational articles for ACSA, the Principal's Network, and LinkedIn.

Adding to her diverse background, Dr. Nash was a small business owner before entering education, bringing a unique perspective to *Lifted to Lead*. Connect with Kathy: linkedin.com/in/dr-kathy-v-nash-5a63219a or kathynash16@gmail.com or go to his website at www.liftedtolead.com

More from ConnectEDD Publishing

Since 2015, ConnectEDD has worked to transform education by empowering educators to become better-equipped to teach, learn, and lead. What started as a small company designed to provide professional learning events for educators has grown to include a variety of services to help educators and administrators address essential challenges. ConnectEDD offers instructional and leadership coaching, professional development workshops focusing on a variety of educational topics, a roster of nationally recognized educator associates who possess hands-on knowledge and experience, educational conferences custom-designed to meet the specific needs of schools, districts, and state/national organizations, and ongoing, personalized support, both virtually and onsite. In 2020, ConnectEDD expanded to include publishing services designed to provide busy educators with books and resources consisting of practical information on a wide variety of teaching, learning, and leadership topics. Please visit us online at connecteddpublishing.com or contact us at: info@connecteddpublishing.com

Recent Publications:

Live Your Excellence: Action Guide by Jimmy Casas

Culturize: Action Guide by Jimmy Casas

Daily Inspiration for Educators: Positive Thoughts for Every Day of the Year by Jimmy Casas

Eyes on Culture: Multiply Excellence in Your School by Emily Paschall

Pause. Breathe. Flourish. Living Your Best Life as an Educator by William D. Parker

L.E.A.R.N.E.R. Finding the True, Good, and Beautiful in Education by Marita Diffenbaugh

Educator Reflection Tips Volume II: Refining Our Practice by Jami Fowler-White

Handle With Care: Managing Difficult Situations in Schools with Dignity and Respect by Jimmy Casas and Joy Kelly

Disruptive Thinking: Preparing Learners for Their Future by Eric Sheninger

Permission to be Great: Increasing Engagement in Your School by Dan Butler

Daily Inspiration for Educators: Positive Thoughts for Every Day of the Year, Volume II by Jimmy Casas

The 6 Literacy Levers: Creating a Community of Readers by Brad Gustafson

The Educator's ATLAS: Your Roadmap to Engagement by Weston Kieschnick

In This Season: Words for the Heart by Todd Nesloney, LaNesha Tabb, Tanner Olson, and Alice Lee

Leading with a Humble Heart: A 40-Day Devotional for Leaders by Zac Bauermaster

Recalibrate the Culture: Our Why…Our Work…Our Values by Jimmy Casas

Creating Curious Classrooms: The Beauty of Questions by Emma Chiappetta

Crafting the Culture: 45 Reflections on What Matters Most by Joe Sanfelippo and Jeffrey Zoul

Improving School Mental Health: The Thriving School Community Solution by Charle Peck and Dr. Cameron Caswell

Building Authenticity: A Blueprint for the Leader Inside You by Todd Nesloney and Tyler Cook

Connecting Through Conversation: A Playbook for Talking with Kids by Erika Bare and Tiffany Burns

The Dream Factory: Designing a Purposeful Life by Mark Trumbo

Stories Behind Stances: Creating Empathy Through Hearing "The Other Side" by Chris Singleton

Happy Eyes: Becoming All Things to All People by Ryan Tillman

The Generative Age: Artificial Intelligence and the Future of Education by Alana Winnick

Recalibrate the Culture: Action Guide by Jimmy Casas

Leading with PEOPLE: A Six Pillar Framework for Fruitful Leadership by Zac Bauermaster

A School Leader's Guide to Reclaiming Purpose by Frederick C. Buskey

Foundations of an Elite Culture: Building Success with High Standards and a Positive Environment by David Arencibia

Personalize: Meeting the Needs of All Learners by Eric Sheninger and Nicki Slaugh

The Five Principles of Educator Professionalism: Rebuilding Trust in Schools by Nason Lollar

Words on the Wall: Culturizing Your Classroom For Observable Impact by Jimmy Casas and Cale Birk

School of Engagement: 45 Activities to Ignite Student Learning by Jonathan Alsheimer

Intentional Instructional Moves: Strategic Steps to Accelerate Student Learning by Sherry St. Clair

Overcoming Education: Complex Challenges, Difficult People, and the Art of Making a Difference by Brad R. Gustafson

The Language of Behavior: A Framework to Elevate Student Success by Charle Peck and Joshua Stamper

Whose Permission Are You Waiting For? An Educator's Guide to Doing What You Love by William D. Parker

The Leader You're Not...And Why It's Just As Important As the Leader You Are by Scott Borba

The Growth-Minded Leader by Tyler Cook

Day by Day: 180 Days of Hope and Encouragement by Zac Bauermaster

Make Your Move: For Ambitious People Ready to Live Their Aspirations by Marlon Styles, Jr.

The Hidden Work: What Separates Top Performers From Underachievers by Weston Kieschnick

www.ingramcontent.com/pod-product-compliance
Lightning Source LLC
Chambersburg PA
CBHW060418130626
46555CB00005B/2115